MO… CONQUERORS

abeka
Pensacola, FL 32523-9100
an affiliate of PENSACOLA CHRISTIAN COLLEGE®

Join the ranks of valiant **VICTORS** as they overcome **FEARS**, defeat **DISTRACTIONS**, vanquish **DOUBTS**, and ultimately become

To Teachers and Parents

As students read the adventures found in this book, they will find countless examples of courage. This collection of inspiring pieces features classic authors such as Rudyard Kipling and Louisa May Alcott, as well as modern favorites including Max Lucado and Marguerite Henry. Woven throughout these adventures is a review of the literary concepts that have been highlighted in the Grade 5 Reading Program. As students read, they will cement the concepts they have learned throughout the year and be encouraged to become the conquerors God has created them to be.

Note: The Abeka Reading Program contains selections appropriate for each grade level, typifying specific literary genres written by a diverse range of authors. Selections have been carefully chosen to meet academic standards and to deepen students' understanding of literature. A selection's inclusion is based on literary merit and does not imply an endorsement of the author's worldview or of every work by the author. Throughout this anthology, students are guided to evaluate each selection through a biblical worldview as they encounter many true-to-life situations in literature.

More Than Conquerors

Staff Credits

Managing Editor: Amy Yohe
Product Manager: Barbie Tupua
Editors: Juliane Roberts, Rachel Grosnick, Dawn Mereness, Ana Schriever
Contributors: Jennifer Odom, Cheryl Reid, Bethany Urbina, Siera Weber
Designer: Ruth Ann Chappell
Cover Illustrator: Jeremy Gorman
Illustrators: Brian Jekel, Joshua Burylo, Jamieson Jekel, Jeremy Gorman, Thalia Alvarez, Nathan Black, Abby Fabrizio, Abeka Staff

Credits appear on p. 209, which is considered an extension of copyright page.

Cataloging Data

More than conquerors -- 1st ed.
209 p. : col. ill. ; 22 cm
(Abeka reading program)
ISBN 978-1-63223-328-8
1. Readers (Elementary) 2. Reading (Elementary)
III. Abeka Book, Inc.

Library of Congress: PE1119 .M67 2025
Dewey System: 428.6

CONTENTS

OVERCOMING FEAR WITH COURAGE

Defeating Distraction with Purpose

Conquering Doubt with Trust

Pronunciation Key

Symbol	Example	Symbol	Example
ā	āte	ŏ	nŏt
â	dâre	oi	boil
ă	făt	o͞o	fo͞od
ä	fäther	o͝o	bo͝ok
ə	ago (ə•gō′)	ou	out
ē	ēven	th	thin
ĕ	ĕgg	th	there
ẽ (ər)	pondẽr	tū	pictūre
ī	īce	ū	ūnit
ĭ	ĭt	û	hûrt
ō	ōver	ŭ	ŭp
ô	côrd, taught, saw	zh	measure

Introducing *More Than Conquerors*

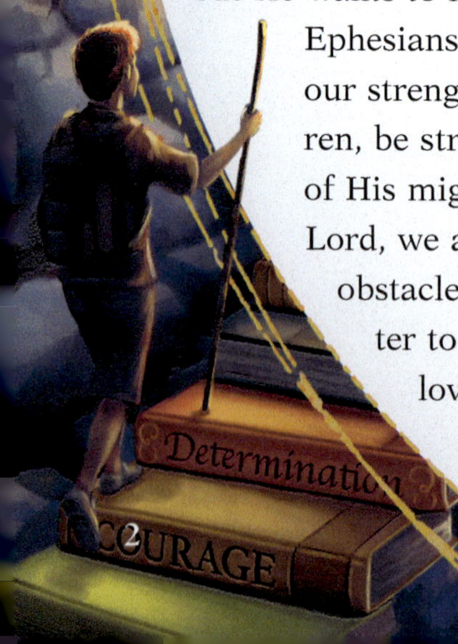

Don't you enjoy a good story? An interesting plot and relatable characters capture our attention and keep us wondering. The author uses the setting, mood, and imagery to keep the reader turning the pages. However, it's ultimately the conflict that keeps the reader reading. When characters have a challenge to face, an obstacle to overcome, or a conflict to resolve, the curious reader wants to reach the climax and the conclusion of the narrative. Without the conflict, nothing interesting would happen in the story; the story would not come to life; and the characters would not experience any development or growth.

Like the characters in many of the stories in *More Than Conquerors*, our lives present challenges to overcome. Without these obstacles, our own character would not experience growth. The child of God has nothing to fear when facing challenges. God is all-powerful and can overcome every problem we face, but He wants to help *us* learn to overcome them. Ephesians 6:10 reminds us where we will find our strength to do this. "Finally, my brethren, be strong in the Lord, and in the power of His might." As we find our strength in the Lord, we also understand that conflicts and obstacles are meant to develop our character to make us more like Him—a follower of Christ who shines the love of God wherever our story takes us.

Good Timber

Douglas Malloch

The tree that never had to fight
For sun and sky and air
and light,
That stood out in the open plain,
And always got its share of rain,
Never became a forest king
But lived and died a scrubby thing.

The man who never had to toil
To gain and farm his patch of soil,
Who never had to win his share
Of sun and sky and light and air,
Never became a manly man
But lived and died as he began.

Good timber does not grow with ease;
The stronger wind, the tougher trees,
The farther sky, the greater length,
The more the storm, the more
the strength:
By sun and cold, by rain and snow,
In tree or man good timbers grow.

Where thickest stands the forest growth,
We find the patriarchs of both.
And they hold converse with the stars
Whose broken branches show
the scars
Of many winds and much of strife.
This is the common law of life.

The Climb

Cheryl Reid

Life in the mountains always offered exciting things to do with every season: skiing in the winter, camping in the spring, rafting in the summer, and hiking in the fall. Ryan loved the outdoors, but he had always been fearful of the sport his Uncle Mark loved most—rock climbing. For Ryan's birthday last week, his uncle had given him climbing gear and promised to teach him about the sport.

Ryan was grateful for the gift and glad that his uncle wanted to spend time with him, but every time he thought about rock climbing, he felt uneasy. Ryan decided to watch some climbing tutorials, hoping that seeing all the safety precautions that climbers put into place would give him some confidence. But Ryan kept thinking of all the things that could go wrong. First, he imagined himself dangling upside down, and then he imagined getting tangled in the ropes.

"At some point," his dad said, "you need to either decide you're ready, or tell your uncle that you just aren't interested in rock climbing. I'm sure he'll understand. But remember, doing hard things can be good for you."

Ryan didn't want to disappoint Uncle Mark, and he didn't want to look back on this opportunity with regret that he was too afraid to try. He decided to call his uncle and let him know that he was ready to learn. They chose next Thursday since fewer people would be at the beginner area than on a Saturday. As the day neared, Ryan tried not to think about being suspended in the air, dependent on a thin rope to keep him from falling to the ground. He knew that his uncle was an expert climber and that he would use every precaution available, but the same fear still nagged at him.

Early Thursday morning, Uncle Mark and Ryan headed to a rock-climbing area at Lookout Mountain especially suited for beginners. "My friend Tyler will meet us there. He's a pro and knows Lookout Mountain like the back of his hand. Sure, there are a couple of challenging areas," his uncle admitted, "but today's climb should be fairly easy if you follow instructions."

Tyler met the pair in the parking lot, and together, the trio hiked the ridge toward the base of the mountain. To Ryan's great relief, the beginner climbing area was deserted. If he were going to make dumb mistakes, he didn't want anyone else to see them. After getting his own gear on, Uncle Mark showed Ryan how to wear his harness and connect the ropes that would hold Ryan if he lost his footing. Uncle Mark explained the function of the belay device that served as a brake, controlling the rope as a climber moves up or down.

"I'm your belayer," Tyler explained. "I hold your rope to keep you safe as you climb. I won't let you fall," Tyler reassured. "Stay focused on where you're going, don't look down, and you will get there safely."

Ryan's hands were sweaty as he dusted them with chalk to improve his grip. Tyler made sure Ryan's helmet was on properly and checked that his climbing shoes were securely fastened.

"We're going to take our time," Uncle Mark explained. "Watch where I place my hands and feet and do exactly what I do. We aren't going to attempt anything dangerous, but be on guard. One wrong move has felled better climbers than me."

Ryan froze as his uncle began the short climb to the first ledge. As though sensing Ryan's fear, Uncle Mark called down to him. "I know it's a little scary, but just remember, Tyler's got you. One foot in front of the other."

"Tyler's got me," Ryan whispered to himself. Uncle Mark coached him as he slowly inched upward. Ryan mimicked his uncle's movements, ascending the first few feet and keeping his eyes focused upward.

Ryan reached the first ledge and sat down. "So far, so good," he breathed. When he looked below, he realized that he had climbed only about fifteen feet. It had felt more like fifty!

"That's all?" Ryan blurted in dismay. "I thought we were halfway to the top!"

Uncle Mark chuckled. "It's not about how far you go, Ryan. It's about knowing you can climb and climb well. Come on," Uncle Mark stood. "Ready to take on the next ledge?"

To Ryan's surprise, the next part of the climb was not as difficult. He kept his eyes on his uncle and followed his every move. After reaching the second ledge, Ryan looked out over the valley beyond Lookout Mountain where his little town lay. He had never seen it from above. He noticed the way the streets were laid out in a grid pattern and how the tall church steeple seemed to stand guard over the entire town. Ryan felt pretty proud of himself for getting this far in the climb. "I'm doing it! I'm rock climbing!"

"You're doing great!" his uncle agreed. "Let's ascend one more level before we call it a day."

Ryan, feeling more confident about the next part of the ascent, watched as his uncle started climbing. Once again, he placed his hands and feet in his uncle's path. Ryan thought, *I must be getting pretty high*, and for a moment, he took his eyes off his uncle and glanced below. That split second of lost concentration was all it took for Ryan to lose his grip and his footing. He swung outward, spun around, and crashed into the rockface headfirst, bumping his helmet.

"I've got you!" Tyler shouted up at Ryan who was suspended about twenty feet in the air.

In seconds, Uncle Mark was beside him, helping him regain his footing and rappel down to the ground.

Once Ryan's feet touched the ground, Tyler and Uncle Mark were a flurry of movement. "What happened?" Uncle Mark asked.

"I looked down," Ryan confessed, "just for a second. I lost my focus."

Tyler rapidly unhooked Ryan's gear so that he could sit down. "You're okay. Just a little shaken up, yeah?"

Ryan nodded his reply, and Tyler continued, "And now you've had a crash course in the importance of safety equipment."

"That was supposed to be for your next lesson," Uncle Mark joked, "but I guess since you're related to me, you're a fast learner."

Ryan let out a shaky laugh.

Uncle Mark decided that they should not end their day with a bad experience, so he suggested another climb after they took a lunch break. Ryan surprised himself by agreeing. At the end of the second climb, most of Ryan's fear had subsided. Following his uncle closely, he successfully made it to the third ledge and back down again.

"I'm proud of you," Uncle Mark said as they drove home. "You had the courage to attempt something hard. That second climb was amazing! You faced your fear, and you conquered it."

Ryan knew his uncle was right. He realized that facing his fear was giving him the confidence to do hard things. Ryan thanked his uncle when he dropped him off at home, and smiling widely asked, "Same time next week?"

In the Spotlight

Elements of a Narrative

Which elements of a narrative did you find in this selection? Using the word web as a guide, explain your answers.

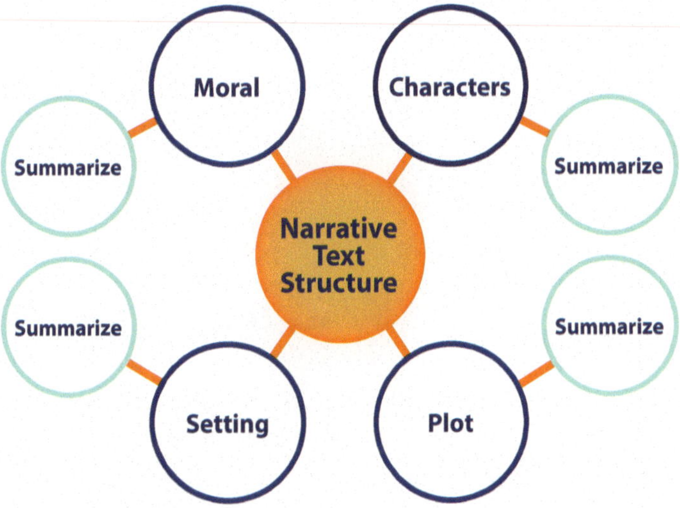

How can we gain victory over fear?

Everyone has a fear of something. Fear is a normal human emotion that serves to warn us when there is real danger. Fear of heights can keep us safe from the real danger of falling, and fear of failure can keep us safe from the perceived danger of embarrassment. Real, imminent danger should never be ignored; but living in fear even when we are safe keeps us from experiencing a full life. Ryan's fear of heights caused him to focus on the *what ifs*, feeding his fear by imagining the worst outcomes. His courageous decision to climb was the first step in overcoming his fear. Ryan took necessary precautions, followed instructions, and accomplished what he had thought was impossible. If Ryan had not decided to try, he would never have known the satisfaction that comes from overcoming fear.

God assures us of His help in any situation. Psalm 31:24 is a good verse to remember when we need to overcome fear with courage. "Be of good courage, and He shall strengthen your heart, all ye that hope in the LORD."

A Race Against Death

from *Perilous Journeys*
by Irma Taylor

Dr. Curtis Welch has seen the number of cases of diphtheria,[1] a highly contagious—and often deadly—disease of the throat, rise daily among his patients. He has nearly run out of the antitoxin which is the only medication that could possibly stop the epidemic. Even if Dr. Welch is able to find some antitoxin somewhere, there seems to be no way to transport the medicine to Nome, Alaska, where it is needed desperately. Nome is a remote town, and it is deepest winter. There is no train to Nome; no ship can cross the frozen sea and reach its harbor; and the bitterly cold weather has made airplane flights impossible. In this story, based on a true event, Dr. Welch and the people of Nome must rely on man's best friend to do what many believe cannot be done.

The pale face of Dr. Curtis Welch grew very serious as he looked about the hospital room. He knew that he faced a hard fight—and all alone! He was the only doctor in the little town of Nome, Alaska, that bitter cold winter in 1925.

Already three babies were dead.

[1] **diphtheria** (dĭf·thîr′ē·ə)

On the hospital beds lay twenty-five sick people. They had diphtheria, a terrible throat disease. If it should get out of control, it would sweep like wildfire over hundreds of square miles. Eleven thousand people were in danger!

A nurse called Dr. Welch to a small bed. "I'm afraid—" she began quietly. A single look told him that one more child was dead.

"We've got to have help," he said in a worried voice. "I mean help from the outside!"

"Yes, it's getting away from us," agreed the nurse. "Maybe some town can send us more doctors. If we were only on the railroad, or if the sea weren't frozen! This load is too much for you alone."

"It is not doctors or nurses we need," said Dr. Welch. "It is medicine. I have hardly five shots of antitoxin left—and that is six years old. Maybe it's no good." He clasped his thin fingers. If he could shoot fresh antitoxin into the arms of the people who were well, they probably would not get sick.

The nurse spoke eagerly, "Can't you radio to the United States for antitoxin?"

"Yes, but it will take six weeks to get here. By that time we may have one of the worst disasters in history."

"But, Doctor, couldn't they reach us sooner with airplanes?" broke in the nurse.

"Not through this weather. No pilot could make it, and it is fifty degrees below zero." The doctor looked very grave. "Our only hope is to get antitoxin from some place closer. Take care of that woman's throat while I call the radio station."

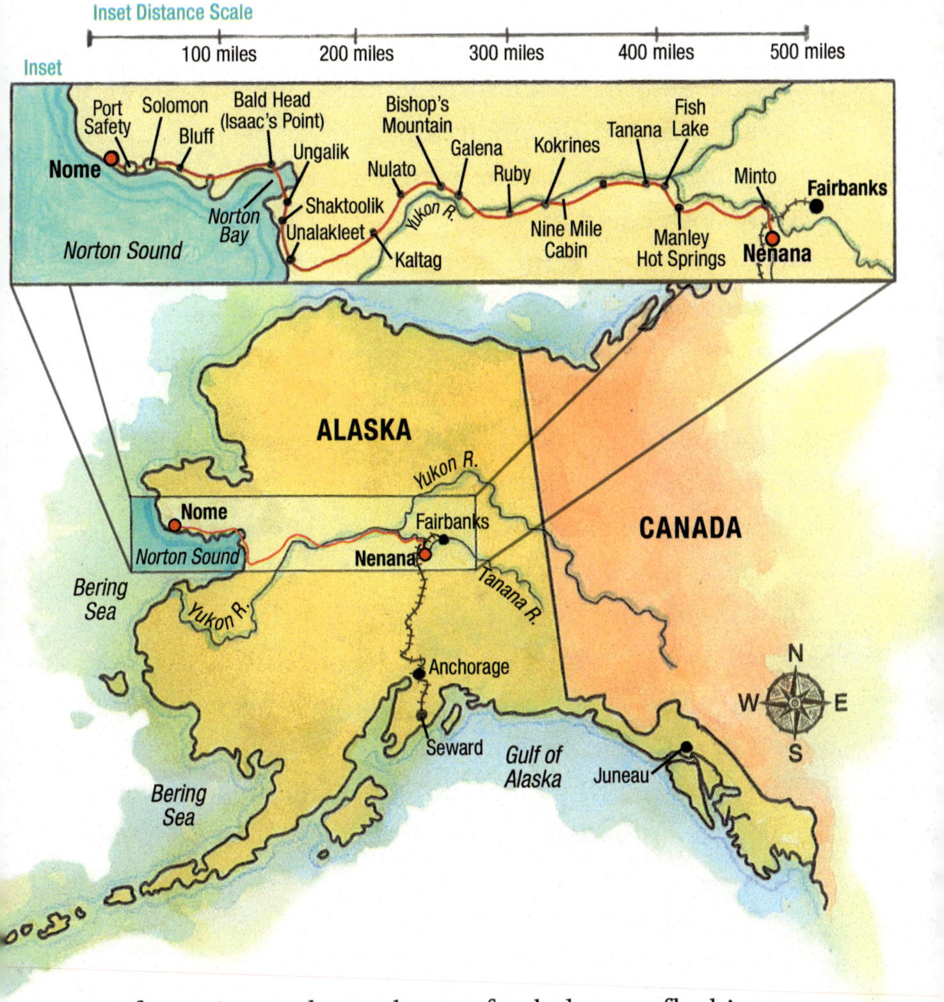

A few minutes later, the cry for help was flashing across the snow. As people heard the bad news, they were much alarmed. Nome was near the Arctic Circle, four hundred miles from the nearest railroad, and frozen in by the sea. Yet help must be sent at once.

A doctor in southern Alaska heard the message. He happened to have a good supply of antitoxin, and immediately wired Dr. Welch: "I am sending antitoxin to Nenana on today's train." Nenana was the town closest to Nome on the railroad.

So the precious twenty-pound package was started on its journey. After the three hundred miles by train, it must be carried six hundred fifty miles over the cruel, snowbound trail stretching between Nenana and Nome.

Only dogs could make it!

Again the radio sent out a call—this time for drivers of dog teams. These drivers are known as mushers, and their dogs are huskies. At once brave mushers picked out their strongest dogs, hitched them to their sleds, and hurried to the trail. The six-hundred-fifty-mile trail had never been covered in less than nine days. But this was a race against death, with eleven thousand lives at stake!

At eleven o'clock on Tuesday evening, January 27, the package on which so many lives depended was taken off the train. The first musher, waiting with his dog team, took it eagerly and set out on the trail.

The great relay race had begun. Each musher would struggle on until he reached the next man, twenty-five to one hundred miles away.

We do not know much about the first heroes who carried the medicine. We know their names and the route they took. But the greatest honor has been paid to the two mushers who bore the most dangerous part of the journey. Of course, their skill and daring would not have been enough. The others had to do their part also, but to these two fell the greatest tests of heroism. Their courage and that of the huskies who led their teams would have been hard to equal.

Shannon was the first musher. Every inch of the trail was familiar to him as he hurried down a frozen stream bed toward the Yukon River. Even in the dark he recognized the dwellings he was passing. He knew he was making good time—more than five miles an hour.

Wednesday noon, Shannon, tired but happy, turned the package over to the second musher. It was time for Shannon to stop because his dogs were worn out. Losing no time, the second stout team plunged down the trail. By seven o'clock in the evening they had reached the Yukon River.

One hundred fifty miles in twenty hours!

If the next teams could only keep up the pace! Just twenty-four hours later, the antitoxin was three hundred fifty miles on its way.

Friday afternoon it was placed in the hands of Leonard Seppala, known far and wide as "the king of dog-team drivers." This daring musher had come out from Nome to meet the medicine. He had covered two hundred miles of difficult trail in four days. Now, with no chance to rest, his picked team of Siberian dogs turned back on the trail.

Seppala hoped to carry the antitoxin all the way back to Nome so that it would get there Saturday afternoon. This would mean covering those two hundred miles in one day! Even in the fresh fallen snow! And with the temperature down below zero.

His team soon came to the edge of the ice-covered Norton Bay. Anxiously he looked out over the frozen surface, for the direct route to Nome lay across this bay. It would be safer to take the land route around it, but that would add almost another hundred miles. If he followed the land, maybe the antitoxin would arrive too late. Seppala decided quickly. It would be the short, dangerous way.

"Gee, Togo!" he cried, and the beautiful forty-eight-pound husky dog headed out over the ice.

The musher watched the sixteen-year-old dog with a thrill of pride. Togo was a natural leader. He was a wonder at picking up the trail, and the other dogs knew they must obey him.

It was now dark. The condition of the ice worried Seppala. Any minute it might break up and drift out to sea. Sometimes, before they had realized the ice was free, travelers have been carried for miles on a loose ice

cake. Some have been blown out into Bering Sea and drowned.

Horrible thoughts crowded into Seppala's mind. *"Suppose the bay ice should suddenly crack up. We would be carried to open water and drift helplessly all night. Nobody could rescue us. My dogs would freeze to death—and so would I—if we did not drown first. And the antitoxin would be lost, somewhere on the bottom of the sea. They trusted it to me, and I must get through."*

Speed—there lay his safety. Togo picked his way carefully as the team raced along. Each husky seemed to know that Seppala was depending upon him. They loved this master who never struck with a whip.

Midnight came. Seppala wondered whether they were halfway across. How cold it was! Didn't he hear a cracking noise? His heart stood still! Togo raced on as if he knew the danger.

At last the sky turned gray. The musher looked eagerly for signs of land. Ahead lay only an icy stretch.

No, wasn't that a shadowy coast line a bit to the right? A few minutes later, he was sure. Another mile slipped by. They would make it safely—the ice would hold!

"My good dogs!" he cried proudly. "Gee, Togo."

Togo led the team up on the snowy bank—and the treacherous bay ice was left behind. Seppala hummed a little song. Now if this team he loved could only go the rest of the way!

Suddenly, as he rounded a turn, he saw a dog team and musher waiting on the trail. Much as he would have liked to press on himself, he knew it would be wiser to let this fresh team of dogs take over.

"Hello, Olson," he called, stopping his sled beside the new team. "Here is the antitoxin." He smiled cheerfully as he handed over the package to the musher.

"Things are worse in Nome . . . another death!" said Olson. His fingers were busy tying the package to the sled. "You made wonderful time, Seppala."

Olson and his seven dogs were off. Before their twenty-five-mile run was over, these dogs were almost frozen.

With great relief Olson handed the antitoxin to the last musher. Gunnar Kasson, who lived in Nome, had been waiting in an empty cabin for two days and nights. He had not even lain down because he was afraid he might fall asleep and then miss Olson. Thirteen stout-hearted dogs made up his team.

He said to Olson, "I am going to take the antitoxin into the cabin for a few minutes. The terrible wind may have frozen it."

Although the men waited inside the cabin for two hours, the weather kept getting colder. It was thirty degrees below. Snow began to fall. Every time they looked outside, the flakes were pelting down faster. A snowstorm meant dangerous going, Kasson knew. But he said, "There is no use waiting any longer."

Stepping outside, he called his lead dog, "Hey, Balto!"

Thirteen balls of fur scrambled out of their warm nests in the snow.

"Here, Balto. Here, boy!"

A handsome husky with a glossy coat ran to his place at the head of the traces.[2] As Kasson fastened the dog into the harness, he said, "Tonight we'll have a hard pull. We have to make it through, boy!"

---

[2] **traces**—*harness straps that connect an animal to the load he is pulling*

The dog pricked up his ears and raised intelligent eyes as if he understood.

Thirty-four miles away lay the next town, a little place called Safety. They must reach it before snowbanks could pile up and block the trail.

"Mush!" cried Kasson.

The dogs headed out bravely on the trail following the coast. It was terribly hard pulling. Although animals and sled sank into the heavy snow, the team struggled on.

"Whew, I never felt a colder wind!" thought Kasson, trying to pull his long reindeer coat closer around him. Sealskin boots reached to his hips, and over these he wore sealskin trousers. His head was protected by a reindeer hood. But the fierce eighty-mile gale whipped right through the skins.

Their way led straight into the wind. How could he or the dogs face it! He feared they would all freeze to death. Even though they kept going, how long could they stay on the trail?

Something else made Kasson very uneasy. The ice under his feet was in constant motion from ocean ground swells. He turned the dogs in closer to the shore line. Now he was crossing the mouth of a frozen river.

Suddenly he realized that Balto was in trouble.

The lead dog had stepped into a pool of water, an overflow that had run up on the ice. Unless Balto's feet could be dried off immediately, the skin would stick to the ice and be torn off. Then he would have to drop out—and he was the only lead dog in the team. It was a bad moment. Just then Kasson saw the one thing that could save Balto's feet—a snowdrift a few yards away.

"Gee, Balto!" he shouted, and the dog turned sharply to the right.

When Balto felt the soft snow, he knew just what to do. He worked his paws in the snow until they were dry. Now the skin was safe. Kasson breathed a sigh of relief.

Starting off again, he headed the team up a six-hundred-foot hill. Here there was nothing to stop the fury of the wind howling in off the sea. Kasson's lips set tightly. This hill was the spot he feared more than any other. Near the top he discovered that his right cheek had no feeling. It was frozen. He grabbed up some snow and rubbed the cheek until it felt alive again.

He was glad to leave the hill behind. Next came a flat stretch six miles long. He wondered whether they would ever get across it, for the wind was picking up masses of snow and hurling them. Kasson was choked and blinded. He strained to catch sight of the dogs. The dog nearest the sled was not even a blur. He held up his hand—no use, he could not see it!

His heart sank. Lost—he was hopelessly lost. The antitoxin would never reach Nome.

Yet the sled was moving steadily on. There was one hope left—that the dogs could keep the trail themselves. Kasson thought, *"Balto will not fail me!"*

The heroic lead dog never hesitated. Hurrying straight ahead, he scented the trail on the glaring, wind-swept ice. For two hours the musher held to the sled and trusted everything blindly to Balto.

They entered the tiny village of Solomon. Kasson did not even see the cabins. In this village a message was waiting for him: "Stop in Solomon until the storm clears. Then go on to Safety. Ed Rohn is there with a fresh team. Let him finish the race."

Kasson sped on through the storm, not knowing he had passed Solomon—not dreaming he had missed an important message.

If anything, the wind grew more bitter in the next twelve miles. Kasson was filled with joy when finally he caught sight of an old log store. He was in the village of Safety. His wonderful Balto had followed the trail!

Kasson saw that all the houses were dark. Not knowing that another musher was waiting here, he thought, "Shall I stop for help? It would mean a long delay. There may not be any dogs in town strong enough to mush through the storm. Balto knows the trail; there is no other dog like him."

Speeding past the dark hotel, the team soon left Safety behind. Just twenty-one miles to go. The trail followed the shore of Bering Sea.

An angry wind whipped in from the sea. "I will tear you off the sled!" it seemed to cry. Kasson clung the tighter.

He was growing very tired. The dogs, too, were slowing up, almost worn out by the long, cruel grind. Deep drifts made the pulling terribly hard. Yet they struggled bravely on. They would reach the goal—or die in the traces!

Kasson was thinking of many things: the rosy flames of a warm fire, how wonderful it would feel when he got to Nome. Would all his dogs make it through? Too bad to lose even one—it must not be Balto! What wouldn't he give for a drink of steaming hot coffee! How far away was Nome? Fifteen miles? Twelve miles? How

many more
sick people had
died? He must
hurry—hurry—

Just then Kasson felt the sled pitch roughly. The next instant, he was flung into the snow. As the sled overturned in a great drift, Balto slowed down and stopped the team. The dogs began to bark and fight, tangling up their harness.

Kasson jumped up and put the sled back on both runners. Then, lashing his whip, he quieted the dogs. It took him some time to straighten their harness in the dark. When they were ready to start again, he reached down to see whether the antitoxin was securely fastened.

What a horrible moment—*the antitoxin was gone*!

Crawling on his hands and knees, he hunted frantically in the snow. The sled had turned over on the right. Surely he would find the metal can there—if he had not lost it miles back on the trail. Could that have happened?

No, thank heaven, here it was!

His heart began to beat again. This time he tied the package very securely.

As they set out, the snowfall seemed lighter. At times he could see a bit of trail ahead. Then in the half-light he saw that two dogs were suffering—the two that had been frozen a few weeks before. The poor creatures were limping stiffly. Stopping the team, he fastened rabbit skin covers over these two dogs, but it didn't help much, for the cold went right through. If they should die, he would leave them and press on. If all the dogs should die, he would still go on, carrying the antitoxin in his arms. Nome—he must get to Nome!

He wished for morning as the hours dragged by. Now he was running behind the sled, for the team was staggering.

"Keep going, Balto," he cried. "We're almost there!" It seemed the team could not last another mile.

He was straining his eyes looking for the lumber mill at the edge of Nome.

At last it appeared out of the falling snow. Thank God, they had made it—they had made it to Nome! It was 5:36 in the morning of Monday, February 2—just five and a half days after the start at Nenana.

The dogs seemed to know that the end of the great race was near. They hurried past the mill, past a row of wooden houses. Kasson heard people shouting, knew

they were running after him. He turned to the left—there was the hospital. The next thing he knew Dr. Welch was wringing his hand. "You got here in time!" said the doctor joyfully. The crowd shouted.

Half frozen and almost blinded, Kasson dropped down into the snow. With tears in his eyes, he started to pull ice splinters out of Balto's paws.

"Balto!" he cried. "Wonderful dog! You brought us through!"

Driving a team of sled dogs, or mushing, is an age-old Alaskan tradition. Native Alaskans relied on their dog teams for transportation during the long and dark winter months. When the first Europeans arrived, they recognized how useful and reliable dog power could be. Mushers delivered the U.S. mail. They brought supplies into remote villages and transported gold from the mining boomtowns. Togo and Balto led their teams through unbelievably harsh conditions to bring the life-saving serum to Nome. When Kasson was blinded by the swirling snow, Balto led the team by scent. Seppala and his team, led by Togo, covered the longest and the most dangerous part of the run, at one point braving temperatures as low as 85°F below zero. Without the deeds of these mushers and their dogs, many more people in Nome would have perished that winter.

In the Spotlight

Elements of a Plot

Using the diagram as a guide, summarize the elements of the plot.

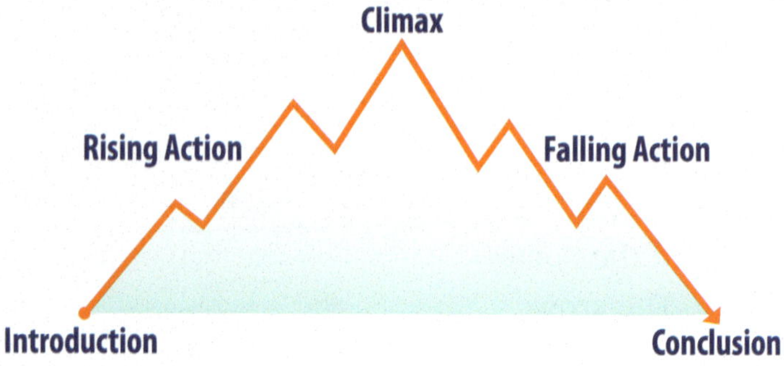

I WONDER . . .

1. Which genre is represented in this selection?
   a. drama b. poetry c. prose
2. Describe the setting for this selection.
3. How does the setting contribute to the mood?
4. How does the mood change during the falling action?

Think on These Things

During the diphtheria outbreak in Nome, several mushers and their dog teams overcame desperate odds to deliver antitoxin before the disease could spread. Their actions saved thousands of lives. What would motivate a person to risk his or her life for others?

When God breathed into the first man, He gave the gift of life. Each person is created in the image of God and is precious to Him. Psalm 127:3 tells us that each new life is His reward. John 15:13 says, "Greater love hath no man than this, that a man lay down his life for his friends." Jesus demonstrated supreme love when He laid down His life for us. Understanding His love causes us to consider others and not just ourselves. Love transforms fear into courage and despair into hope.

 To focus on Map Skills, see page 203.

The Fighting Red Tails:
America's First Black Airmen

Warren Halliburton

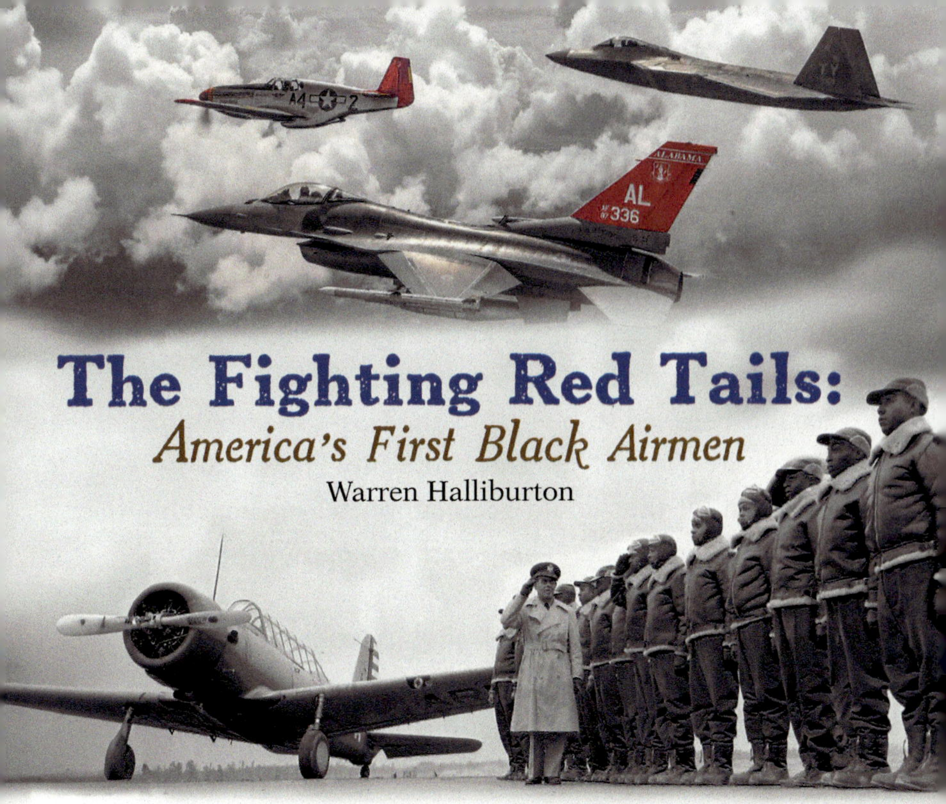

"The Fighting Red Tails" is a historical account of the first Black American pilots and their brave exploits during World War II. Before the 1940s, Black American soldiers were not allowed to become pilots. The brave squadrons set aside personal injustices for the privilege of defending freedoms not yet realized for all Americans. The 332nd Fighter Group was formed when several squadrons of the Tuskegee airmen came together under the command of an inspiring leader, Colonel Benjamin O. Davis, Jr. The tails of their P-51 Mustangs were painted red to make them easily identifiable as they escorted bombers into enemy territory. The "Red Tails" became famous for their courage and tenacity.

All through the month of June 1944, the 332nd flew with the bombers of the 15th Air Force. The bombing targets were in Italy, southern France, and the Balkans.[1]

[1] **Balkans**—*Greece and countries that surround the Balkan Peninsula*

It seemed that they were meeting enemy planes on every bombing run. Each battle was worse than the last, and more and more pilots of the 332nd were lost. The enemy seemed to know the Americans were losing. They fought that much harder, sending new planes to stop the Americans from knocking out their supply lines.

Just west of Aircasea,[2] Italy, was a strip of landing ground believed to be one of the Nazi's most important air supply lines. The American army knew that Italy would fall if they could keep supplies from reaching the enemy's front lines. The job of wiping out the supply lines fell to the 332nd.

The American air attack had to be done in a special way, for if the enemy learned of it, they would be able to find the P-47 fighters almost immediately. A giant radar network along the Italian coast protected the Nazis against just such attacks. The 332nd Squadron had only one way

[2] **Aircasea** (âr·cŏs′ē·ə)

to keep from being spotted. That was to fly low—too low to be picked up by radar. There was no doubt that the plan was dangerous, but it was the only way to get the job done.

On June 24, the Black fighter squadron took off, skimming low over the waters of the Mediterranean Sea. The weather was bad; thick, dark clouds blotted out the sunlight.

Suddenly, the engine of one plane cut out, and the plane dipped into the water. Pulling back on his stick, the pilot lifted his plane. But the engine failed to catch, and the P-47 nosed back down and crashed. It sank almost immediately.

Every man in the group watched in horror, but the 332nd continued on. Now and then a giant wave lashed upward toward the low-flying airplanes. Suddenly another plane slipped too low and was slapped at by the waves. When the pilot tried to pull up, he discovered that the weight of the fuel and bombs made his plane sluggish.

A wing was ripped by water. The pilot jumped out just before the plane skidded and crashed, luckily escaping the quickly sinking craft.

One of the other pilots spotted the man in the sea and went after him in a tight 180-degree turn. A downward gust of air caught his plane, throwing it into a flat spin. A moment later the plane exploded as it hit the sea. Neither pilot could be seen through the thick, heavy smoke that covered the water.

By this time the 332nd was halfway to its target—but its problems were by no means over. The lead pilot had made a mistake. He had turned east at the place where he should have turned north. Reaching the coast, the planes were more than 70 miles from where they should have been. The lead pilot saw his mistake and made a 90-degree turn.

He evidently was closer to the water than he thought because all of a sudden he saw the water rush up toward him. But it was too late. All at once the plane plunged into the waves and a moment later the giant explosion it made lifted the sea. No trace of the plane was to be seen. The radio was still. No one said a word as the assistant flight leader moved forward to take the lead.

At last the planes were close to the target. But now a thick fog began to roll in, and the pilots could not see the ground below them. As they closed in on the Nazi supply strip, the fog got thicker. Nothing could be seen of the enemy. The new flight leader made a painful decision.

"Give it up! Give up the target. We're going home!" he called into the radio.

This was a terrible blow to the pilots of the 332nd. Four good men already had lost their lives on this flight—and for nothing. The enemy had not even been touched!

The next day, the pilots of the 332nd answered the call from Flight Operations. Their hearts were heavy, but every man knew the flight had to go on. Their job this time was some low-flying bombing of roads in northern Italy, known to be the enemy's main supply lines for the fighting further south. If they were destroyed, much of the enemy's strength would be cut.

The 332nd went to work. Although no one said it, each man wanted to lash back with greater effort today at what happened yesterday, thinking that perhaps he could somehow make up for the loss of four friends.

The winds were strong and blew against them—stronger than they had expected. Even though the weather was clear, the planes were blown off course into German sea lanes. An enemy ship was now filling the skies with antiaircraft fire. One pilot said later, "It was so thick . . . it looked like a blanket."

In screaming dives, the planes of the 332nd opened up with all guns on the shell-spitting Nazi destroyer. Before long they had the ship ablaze with fire and smoke. Then another direct hit and the enemy ship blew up.

The news of this victory at sea went everywhere. While it was cheered wherever it was heard, the men of the 332nd Fighter Group took their fame with quiet pleasure. These men were no longer eager young boys. Yes, they had now come back from the blow of defeat and had scored a major victory!—but they were not wild with joy. For now every man in the group was remembering four friends flying with them just one day before.

It was clear by July 1944 that Nazi Germany was losing the war. Total defeat was closer every day. The Nazis were fighting harder than ever to keep back the advance of the Allied armies, but theirs was a losing battle. American leaders had planned well.

Just when the war was going well, the 332nd found it had a new kind of trouble. This time it was not trouble from the enemy; it came from within. By now the attacks on Germany's oil fields were in full force. The 332nd was moved to Rametti,[3] Italy, where they were

---

[3] **Rametti** (rə·mĕt′ē)

joined by the famous 99th Fighter Squadron—the first Black air squadron in the history of the U.S. Army. The 99th was to become part of the 332nd, making the all-Black fighter force bigger and stronger.

But the change was not that easy to make, for the pilots of the 99th had fought long and well in the war and did not want to belong to a group of flyers they thought were still young and untried.

The men of the 332nd had their own problems with the change. True, they had not fought as much as the 99th, but they felt they were just as able. Slowly but surely, the new and bigger 332nd split into two unfriendly camps.

Col. Davis saw what was happening. He knew that unless his men worked together they could not fight well. This kind of problem could be more dangerous for the 332nd Fighter Group than the enemy. He understood that working out the problem would be up to him.

He convinced the men that the only reason they were there was to fight and win the war. They were trained fighter pilots and their one job was to destroy the enemy, not one another.

The men of the 332nd got the message and they took comfort. Their number had grown, the group had gained experience, and now they could all see that they had to work together to win.

All this time the enemy was hard at work—fixing what weapons they could still use to fight, setting up new lines of supply, and building new supply stations in different places. These stations now had to be destroyed by the Allies. The American bombers went out on raids seventeen days a month. The new 332nd went along on many of these missions, fighting off groups of enemy planes sent to destroy the B-24 bombers over Rumania,[4] Austria, and Bohemia.[5]

The men of the 332nd came back from each mission with a new story and a new hero. One such hero was Captain Joseph D. Elsberry, a young officer who always seemed ready to go into battle. Three Nazi pilots found this out about him the morning of July 12. Captain Elsberry was leading a fighter group that day whose job was protecting American bombers. Elsberry spotted enemy planes coming in and radioed his men to prepare their ships for a fight, which meant dropping their extra fuel. The planes could move better in a fight if they were lighter.

By this time the P-47s had dropped back. The bombers went on alone to finish their mission. The Nazis, seeing the gas tanks falling from the fighter planes and thinking the small planes were dropping bombs, turned away from the bombers and started after the fighters instead.

The Nazi pilots made their move a moment too late, though. By the time they turned away from the bombers, the 332nd fighter pilots, led by Capt. Elsberry, were already on their tails.

The captain lined up his gun sight and fired a short burst. Although the side of one Nazi plane blew away, Elsberry kept on its tail. He fired again; the enemy plane went out of control, slipped off to the right, and fell to the earth.

A moment later a second enemy plane flashed by. Elsberry rolled his plane in a steep turn and started

---

[4] **Rumania**—*modern-day Romania*
[5] **Bohemia**—*modern-day Czech Republic*

firing. The Nazi plane began to smoke, fell into a dive, and plunged to the ground.

As he pulled out of his turn, Elsberry caught sight of another enemy plane. As it quickly shot across his path in a sharp dive, Elsberry rolled to his left and went after the plane. Then he started firing. The Nazi twisted and turned the plane to avoid Elsberry. He was a good pilot, but not as good as the American.

The Nazi pilot continued his dive. Down he went, hoping to avoid the American on his tail. Just before reaching the ground he tried to pull out of his dive. It was too late. The plane crashed into the ground, leaving a ball of fire to mark the spot where it hit the green land below.

By the end of the month almost all the enemy's oil fields had been bombed by the Allies. Soon there was not even half the oil the Nazi army needed for fuel. This was the beginning of the end for Hitler's Germany. And hints of the next big step were in the air. The Allies would invade Germany itself.

"Destroy everything that moves!" was the order. "We are moving into Germany."

The job for the 332nd was to finish their work as well as they had started it. Their days together from the time they were eager young cadets had brought them down a long, hard path. Many had been lost on the way, but those who were left knew that they would now set the stage for the biggest part in the war. An invasion by Allied ground troops was around the corner. And then—*the end of the war*!

The day came when the 332nd was given time out from fighting. There was something going on—something special. Everyone could feel it and the men shared the feeling with winks and grins. Then the official word came from army chiefs in Washington, D.C. On September 10, four pilots of the fighter group were to get awards for all they had done in service to their country.

The day was to be special in another way. Col. Benjamin O. Davis, Jr., was also to be honored. And General Benjamin O. Davis, Sr., his father, was flying in to present the awards. The general was the highest ranking Black officer in the U.S. Army.

The men of the 332nd were all "spit-and-polish" as the ceremony began. All eyes were on Gen. Davis. Smartly marching up to the stand, he spoke to his son.

"I am very proud of you," he said.

Everyone there felt something special pass between father and son. Both had a look in their eyes that everyone understood. Then the general went on to read the army's message to the men of the 332nd.

FOR EXTRAORDINARY ACHIEVEMENT IN AN AERIAL FLIGHT AS PILOT OF A P-47 TYPE AIRCRAFT. FACED WITH THE PROBLEM OF PROTECTING THE LARGER BOMBER FORMATION WITH THE COMPARATIVELY FEW FIGHTERS UNDER HIS CONTROL, COL. DAVIS SO SKILLFULLY DISPOSED[6] HIS SQUADRON THAT THE BOMBER FORMATION SUFFERED FEW LOSSES.

The following four men of the 332nd also got awards that day:

CAPT. ALFONSO DAVIS: HE LED AN ATTACK ON AN ENEMY AIRFIELD AT GROZWARDIN,[7] RUMANIA, ON AUGUST 30. THE 332ND DESTROYED 83 PLANES ON THE GROUND IN THIS RAID.

CAPT. JOSEPH D. ELSBERRY: BATTLED HIS WAY TO HIS TARGETS, DEFEATING THE ENEMY IN THE AIR AND DESTROYING HIS VITAL INSTALLATION ON THE GROUND.

FIRST LIEUTENANT CLARENCE D. LESTER: WITH COMPLETE DISREGARD FOR HIS PERSONAL SAFETY HE DESTROYED THREE ENEMY FIGHTERS, THUS PREVENTING THE ENEMY FROM MAKING CONCENTRATED ATTACKS ON THE BOMBERS.

LIEUTENANT JACK D. HOLSCLAW: WITH COMPLETE DISREGARD FOR HIS PERSONAL SAFETY . . . WITH AN OUTSTANDING DISPLAY OF DARING AND COMBAT SKILL, DESTROYED TWO ENEMY FIGHTERS AND FORCED THE REMAINDER TO BREAK OFF THEIR ORGANIZED ATTACKS.

Every man of the 332nd took satisfaction in these awards. They understood that the honors given to their friends were very much their own. Each man knew he had done his share.

---

[6] **disposed**—*arranged or set up*

[7] **Grozwardin** (grōz·vär′dĭn)

And the men of the 332nd continued to do their share throughout the rest of the war in Europe. Finally, at midnight on May 8, 1945, the fighting in Europe was over. The Allies had beaten the Nazis. The bloodshed and killing on European battlefields and in the air had ended.

And then, once again, on June 8, 1945, Col. Benjamin Davis was honored. This time he was given the Silver Star for bravery in combat. The commanding general of the 15th Air Force said of Col. Davis: *He is a fine soldier and has done wonders with the 332nd. I am positive that no other man in our air corps could have handled this job in the manner he has.*

The 332nd had been overseas for 22 months. During that time 450 Black pilots had joined its ranks. They flew nearly 1,600 missions and over 15,000 air flights. They had proven that color was not important among fighting soldiers. No one race of people owned the will or courage to fight bravely and win. Nor did any one race of people own a love for their country.

On October 17, 1945, the fighter group was awarded the Presidential Distinguished Unit Citation, the highest award that can be given to an army unit.

Their skill and daring made all the Red Tails outstanding as pilots and as Americans. They cut a path of honor for those who would follow in America's fighting forces.

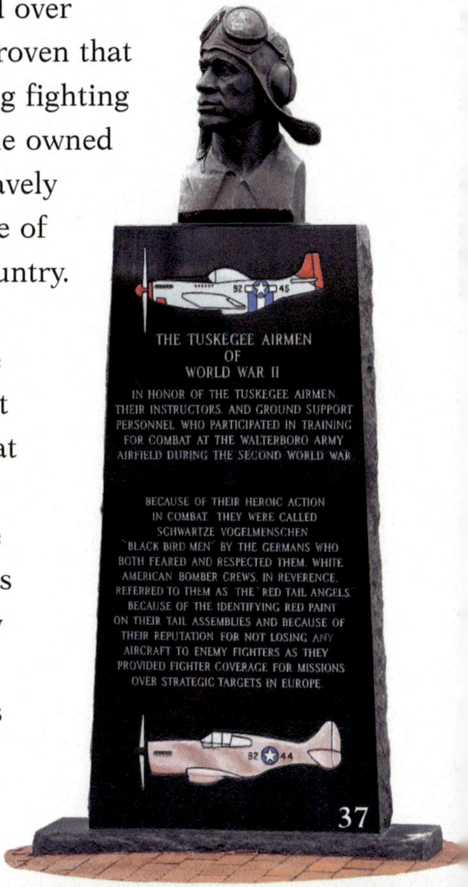

I WONDER . . .

Using the timeline below, answer the following questions.

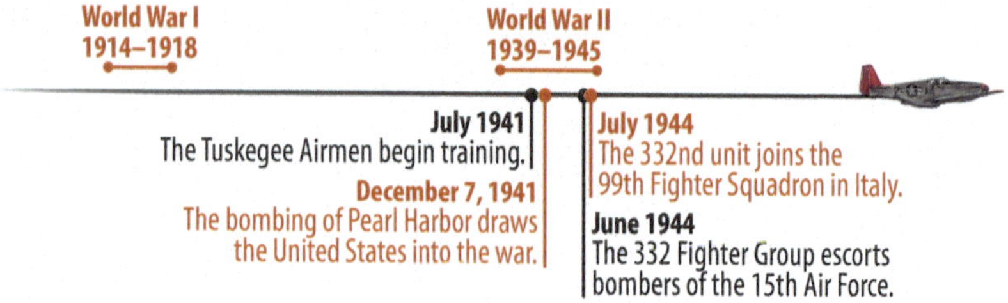

1. During which war do these events take place?
2. When were the Tuskegee Airmen allowed to begin training as pilots?
3. On June 24, 1944, when targeting a Nazi destroyer, what daring strategy did the pilots of the 332nd use?
4. How did the men of the 332nd react when, the day after they lost four friends, they had to return to their mission?
5. At what point in time did American leaders realize that Nazis in Germany were losing the war?
6. What did Col. Davis do that showed he was a wise leader?
7. Many individual pilots were recognized for their achievements. What does the response of the group tell you about the character of the men and Col. Davis's success in making them into one cohesive unit?

Because of their willingness to set aside differences and injustices, the brave Red Tails "cut a path of honor for those who would follow." What does this mean?

CHARACTER

Margaret Slattery

What one *is*, *that* is the supreme thing. Sincerity, honesty, unselfishness, intelligence, the spirit of cooperation and justice, cheerfulness, courtesy, concentration, and all the rest help make one what he is. What one *is*—that is Character. Strong, fine character stands the test of life with all its dangers and pitfalls—nothing else does.

Everyone has the power of making his character what it ought to be. The power lies in the little words "Yes" and "No." Saying "Yes" to all that life offers which is good and right and saying "No" to all that can weaken or defile will form character strong, pure, and fine.

Think on These Things

1. How does the author define character?
2. True or False: You are born with the character that you will have all your life.
3. How can you develop good character?

"He that walketh uprightly walketh surely: but he that perverteth his ways shall be known." —Proverbs 10:9

Ross Carson's Courage

Author Unknown

Do you ever feel as if you are the only one who experiences problems and that no one else understands what you are going through? You might be surprised to find out that your problem is more common than you think. In this fictional narrative, what challenge does Ross Carson face that requires courage?

Shouting, laughing, pushing against each other, the boys rushed out of the schoolhouse pell-mell.

"Look out, Ross Carson," shouted Tom Lane, in a tone of pretended alarm, "there's a spider on the pump handle. Run quick, it may bite you."

There was a roar of laughter at this would-be witty remark, and the eyes of a score or more thoughtless boys were bent upon the figure of a slender, frail-looking lad who had been one of the first to get out and who had approached the pump for the purpose of getting a drink.

His face flushed painfully as Tom's jest[1] fell on his ear, and the hand that held the tin drinking cup trembled perceptibly,[2] and his lips scarcely touched the water.

"Oh, he'll stand anything rather than double up his little fist," cried Tom, and crowding close to Ross, he deliberately knocked the books from under his arm. The slender lad's face flushed at the insult, but he said

---

[1] **jest**—*mocking remark*

[2] **perceptibly**—*noticeably*

nothing. He stooped, picked the books up, and then walked on again.

He was quite aware of Tom Lane's great desire to pick a quarrel with him, but was determined to give him no excuse for doing so. For Ross knew that he could not with safety enter into any trial of strength with a boy so much older than himself. His lungs were weak, and the doctor had said they could bear no strain. But it was hard to be called a coward, to bear insults of every description without open resentment, to feel that he was looked upon with contempt[3] by his companions because no taunts or sneers could induce him to fight. And he was too sensitive and shy to explain to them his reasons for not doing so, knowing well that his explanation would be greeted with ridicule and laughter. So he bore his various trials in silence, and not even his mother knew what he endured.

He did not know that this forbearance[4] showed that he possessed true heroism; for like most boys, he had

[3] **contempt**—*disrespect and anger*
[4] **forbearance**—*tolerance*

a strong admiration for deeds of daring and saw little merit in silent endurance.

Tom Lane was the most daring boy among them all. He boasted that he had the coolest head, the strongest arm, and the greatest amount of courage of any fellow of his age in Hillsboro; and none disputed[5] his claim. He was always ready for a fight, and generally came off victor in any contest. He had no pity for weakness, no charity for timidity, and thought all those who feared him fair game for his powers of teasing. Ross might have been fairly treated by the other students, but for Tom, who was never weary of exciting enmity against him, and knowing how to magnify the smallest trifles, was always showing Ross up as "the biggest coward in Hillsboro Academy."

But retribution[6] was near at hand.

A new town hall was being built in Hillsboro; and a very high, imposing[7] structure it was to be with a steeple second to none. Tom Lane heard his father, who was the contractor for the building, say that a magnificent view could be obtained from this half-completed steeple, and the next day at the noon recess, Tom proposed to half a dozen of his young friends to go up and take a look for themselves.

"I have a pass from Father," he said, "and the carpenters won't make any fuss."

The ascent to the steeple was easily made, for narrow, winding stairs led up to it; and the boys soon attained a height that made their heads swim as they looked down, breathless, and saw how small appeared the people on the pavement below.

---

[5] **disputed**—*argued*
[6] **retribution**—*payment*
[7] **imposing**—*having a large and powerful appearance*

"Do be careful," said a low voice in a tone of entreaty,[8] and looking around, the boys saw Ross Carson standing near. He had come up the stairs unnoticed.

"Why are you here, you little coward?" asked Tom rudely.

"I was hoping to see the view with you, but now I can see this is a dangerous place," answered Ross, quietly.

"It's likely you think so," sneered Tom. "You'd find the head of a barrel a dangerous place. As for me, I'd like to see the place where I wouldn't go! Boys, do you see that?"

He pointed to a scaffolding[9] which had been erected about the steeple for the use of the workmen. It projected several feet, and overhung the vast chasm[10] below.

"We see it; but what of it?" asked Louis Raymond.

"You'll see what of it," answered Tom. "It's a jolly place to dance a hornpipe."[11] And before his companions could realize his intention, he had climbed out upon the scaffolding and was walking fearlessly about it.

The boys stared in sheer amazement at such recklessness and begged him to be careful. Their fears for his safety only made Tom more eager to show his boasted courage, and he began rather a feeble imitation of a sailor's hornpipe.

"Wouldn't it be a long jump to the pavement?" Tom said.

As he spoke, he looked down, a fatal thing; for his head, which had until now been so cool and steady, began to whirl strangely. He could not remove his eyes from the awful chasm below him. It seemed to fascinate him.

---

[8] **entreaty**—*an earnest request*
[9] **scaffolding**—*raised platform from which work is done at great heights*
[10] **chasm**—*a deep opening*
[11] **hornpipe**—*a lively dance*

The boys looked at each other in horror. They saw the terrible danger which threatened him. They knew it was only a question of moments now before he would fall. He stood in a kind of daze, looking down into the fascinating gulf, his eyes wild and staring, his face white with terror. He, too, knew the awful danger in which he stood, but he was powerless to help himself. The slightest change of position, even the raising of his eyes, and he would fall. The gulf seemed to be drawing him on; his brain grew more numb with every instant. Back of him shuddered his horror-stricken comrades, waiting

in an agony of suspense for the fatal end of this terrible drama. Before and below him yawned the great chasm, at the bottom of which the people were scarcely seen.

Suddenly there was a movement among the boys, and Ross Carson, with white face and set teeth, climbed quickly and noiselessly out of the steeple onto the scaffolding, and with steady step, approached the boy who stood on the brink of such a fearful death.

"If he touches him, Tom will fall," whispered Louis Raymond.

Low as the whisper was, Ross heard it and half turned his head toward Louis, pausing an instant as if to think. Then he made a quick, firm step forward, and throwing both arms around Tom's waist, dragged him backward.

It was all over in an instant. In the face of a fearful and imminent[12] danger, Ross saved his enemy, and slowly, carefully, for every step was peril, drew him back to the steeple and with the help of the other boys, got him inside once more, trembling, it is true, and utterly unnerved, but safe.

There was little said by anyone. In silence Ross helped Tom descend the winding stair, and then walked home as quickly as possible.

"I don't feel well enough to go to school again this afternoon," Ross said to his mother, "so I'll weed out your flower beds for you."

"You are pale," said Mrs. Carson. "I'm afraid you study too hard."

[12] **imminent**—*about to happen*

Ross did not answer, but threw off his coat and began to weed the beds, hoping by hard work to overcome the nervousness which had possessed him ever since leaving the new town hall. He was still weeding a couple of hours later when he heard the tramp of many feet, and looking up, he saw about a dozen of his schoolmates coming in at the little wooden gate, Tom Lane first of all.

"I've come to ask your forgiveness, Ross Carson," said Tom, holding out his hand. "You've taught me this day what true courage is and made me see what a cowardly sneak I've been."

Tom's lip quivered as he made this humiliating confession, and his eyes were moist with the tears which he could restrain with only the greatest effort. Ross took the outstretched hand in a warm and hearty grasp as he said, "I'd have done as much for anyone, Tom. Don't make so much of it. But I'm glad to be friends with you."

And friends, fast and true, they were from that time forth; and no one ever again even whispered that Ross Carson lacked courage.

The story of that brave deed of his on the scaffolding about the new town hall has borne testimony to his courage which was sufficiently convincing, and the people of Hillsboro were proud of their young townsman. In their eyes, he was a hero. But I think that the noblest thing about his brave act was that he risked his life to save that of his enemy.

Time to Think

1. Why did the students think Ross was a coward?
2. How did Ross demonstrate courage in his first encounter with Tom?
3. What did the line "but retribution was near at hand" foreshadow?
4. How did Tom show courage in the end?

In the Spotlight

Character Analysis

1. How does the author add dimension to Ross's character?
2. Why doesn't the author give us the names of the other boys who follow Tom's example in bullying Ross?
3. In what ways does the author make us believe that Tom is a one-dimensional character?
4. Some characters remain the same throughout the story; others grow and change. What happened to the characters of Ross and Tom by the end of the story?
5. What do you think might happen to the characters of Ross and Tom if the author were to write some more stories about their adventures together?

To focus on Character Development, see page 204.

How can we overcome evil?

Tom's consistently cruel behavior is characteristic of a bully. He never missed a chance to humiliate or threaten Ross, a boy who was younger and not as strong. Tom's behavior was wrong. It would have been natural for Ross to find a way to "get back" at Tom. Yet Ross chose not to do that. Ross even went beyond that by rescuing Tom on the scaffolding. In the end, Tom apologized, admitting in front of the other classmates that he had been a "cowardly sneak," and asked Ross for forgiveness. Ross had overcome evil with good.

This story has a happy ending, with Ross and Tom becoming friends from that day on. In real life, we do not always see the final resolution of the problem of evil. However, when we obey God's commands to return good for evil (Romans 12:21), and to pray for those which despitefully use us (Luke 6:28), we know that we are pleasing Him. We also know that the day will come when evil will be overcome eternally. Until that day, we continue to overcome evil with good.

Life at Plumfield with Jo's Boys

from *Little Men* by Louisa May Alcott

Many of Louisa May Alcott's best-loved books were inspired by her own family and friends. Her most famous book, *Little Women*, is set during the Civil War. It is the story of the four March sisters, who are patterned after Louisa and her own sisters. This selection of narrative fiction is from *Little Men*, the sequel to *Little Women*. Jo—the March sister most like Louisa herself—is now grown up and running a boarding school. As the story opens, Nat Blake arrives at Plumfield for the first time. Nat, who has already overcome much in his short life, hopes he has finally found the place where he belongs. Entering Plumfield, he meets a busy, happy, slightly chaotic group of boys who, like Nat, are orphans but seem to be unlike him in every other way. Will Nat be able to overcome his newest challenge and find a home at last?

"Please, sir, is this Plumfield?" asked a ragged boy of the man who opened the great gate at which the omnibus[1] left him.

[1] **omnibus**—*a horse-drawn wagon used for transporting several passengers, sometimes including an upper deck*

"Yes; who sent you?"

"Mr. Laurence. I have got a letter for the lady."

"All right; go up to the house, and give it to her; she'll see to you, little chap."

The man spoke pleasantly, and the boy went on, feeling much cheered by the words. Through the soft spring rain that fell on sprouting grass and budding trees, Nat saw a large square house before him—a hospitable-looking house, with an old-fashioned porch, wide steps, and lights shining in many windows. Neither curtains nor shutters hid the cheerful glimmer; and, pausing a moment before he rang, Nat saw many little shadows dancing on the walls, heard the pleasant hum of young voices, and felt that it was hardly possible that the light and warmth and comfort within could be for a homeless "little chap" like him.

"I hope the lady *will* see to me," he thought; and gave a timid rap with the great bronze knocker.

A rosy-faced maid opened the door, and smiled as she took the letter which he silently offered. She seemed used to receiving strange boys, for she pointed to a seat in the hall, and said, with a nod,—"Sit there and drip on the mat a bit, while I take this in to missis."

Nat found plenty to amuse him while he waited, and stared about him curiously, enjoying the view, yet glad to do so unobserved in the dusky recess[2] by the door.

The house seemed swarming with boys, who were beguiling[3] the rainy twilight with all sorts of amusements. There were boys everywhere. Various open doors showed pleasant groups of big boys, little boys, and middle-sized

---

[2] **recess**—*a hollow, secluded place*
[3] **beguiling**—*passing time*

boys in all stages of evening relaxation. Two large rooms on the right were evidently schoolrooms, for desks, maps, blackboards, and books were scattered about. An open fire burned on the hearth, and several indolent lads lay on their backs before it, discussing a new cricket[4] field, with such animation that their boots waved in the air. A tall youth was practicing on the flute in one corner, quite undisturbed by the racket all about him. Two or three others were jumping over the desks, pausing, now and then, to get their breath, and laugh at the droll[5] sketches of a little wag[6] who was caricaturing[7] the whole household on a blackboard.

In the room on the left a long supper-table was seen, set forth with great pitchers of new milk, piles of brown and white bread, and perfect stacks of the shiny ginger-bread so dear to boyish souls. A flavor of toast was in the air, also suggestions of baked apples, very tantalizing to one hungry little nose and stomach.

The hall, however, presented the most inviting prospect of all, for a brisk game of tag was going on in the upper entry. One landing was devoted to marbles, the other to checkers, while the stairs were occupied by a boy reading, a girl singing a lullaby to her doll, two puppies, a kitten, and a constant succession of small boys sliding down the banisters, to the great detriment of their clothes, and danger to their limbs.

So absorbed did Nat become in this exciting race, that he ventured farther and farther out of his corner. When one very lively boy came down so swiftly that he

---

[4] **cricket**—*a sport, similar to baseball, played around the world*
[5] **droll**—*comical; humorous*
[6] **wag**—*a witty person*
[7] **caricaturing**—*drawing funny pictures that overemphasize a person's unique qualities*

could not stop himself, he fell off the banisters, with a crash that would have broken any head. Nat forgot himself, and ran up to the fallen rider, expecting to find him half-dead. The boy, however, only winked rapidly for a second, then lay calmly looking up at the new face with a surprised "Hullo!"

"Hullo!" returned Nat, not knowing what else to say.

"Are you a new boy?" asked the youth.

"Don't know yet."

"What's your name?"

"Nat Blake."

"Mine's Tommy Bangs; come up and have a go, will you?" and Tommy got up on his legs like one suddenly remembering the duties of hospitality.

"Guess I won't, until I see whether I'm going to stay or not," returned Nat, feeling the desire to stay increase every moment.

"I say, Demi,[8] here's a new one. Come and see to him;" and the lively Thomas returned to his sport with unabated relish.[9]

At his call, the boy reading on the stairs looked up with a pair of big brown eyes, and after an instant's pause, as if a little shy, he put the book under his arm, and came down to greet the new-comer, who found something very pleasant in the kind face of this slender, mild-eyed boy.

"Have you seen Aunt Jo?" Demi asked, as if that was some sort of important ceremony.

"I haven't seen anybody yet but you boys; I'm waiting," answered Nat.

"Did Uncle Laurie send you?" proceeded Demi, politely, but gravely.

"Mr. Laurence did."

"He is Uncle Laurie; and he always sends nice boys."

Nat looked gratified at the remark, and smiled, in a way that made his thin face very pleasant. He did not know what to say next, so the two stood staring at one another in friendly silence, until the little girl came up with her doll in her arms. She was very like Demi, only not so tall, and had a rounder, rosier face, and blue eyes.

"This is my sister Daisy," announced Demi, as if presenting a rare and precious creature.

The children nodded to one another; and the little girl's face dimpled with pleasure, as she said, pleasantly,—"I hope you'll stay. We have such good times here; don't we, Demi?"

---

[8] **Demi**—*a nickname meaning half-sized*
[9] **unabated relish**—*enjoyment that does not lessen*

"Of course, we do; that's what Aunt Jo has Plumfield for."

"It seems a very nice place indeed," observed Nat, feeling that he must respond to these amiable young persons.

"It's the nicest place in the world; isn't it, Demi?" said Daisy, who evidently regarded her brother as an authority on all subjects.

"No; I think Greenland, where the icebergs and seals are, is more interesting. But I'm fond of Plumfield, and it *is* a very nice place to be in," returned Demi, who was interested just now in a book on Greenland. He was about to offer to show Nat the pictures and explain them, when the maid returned, saying, with a nod toward the parlor-door,—"All right; you are to stay."

"I'm glad; now come to Aunt Jo." And Daisy took him by the hand with a pretty protecting air, which made Nat feel at home at once.

Demi returned to his beloved book, while his sister led the new-comer into a back room, where a stout gentleman was entertaining two little boys on the sofa, and a thin lady was just finishing the letter which she seemed to have been re-reading.

"Here he is, Aunty!" cried Daisy.

"So this is my new boy? I am glad to see you, my dear, and hope you'll be happy here," said the lady, drawing him to her, and stroking back the hair from his forehead with a kind hand and a motherly look, which made Nat's lonely little heart yearn toward her.

She had a merry sort of face, that never seemed to have forgotten certain childish ways and looks, any more than her voice and manner had; and these things, hard to describe but very plain to see and feel, made her a comfortable kind of person, easy to get along with, and generally "jolly," as boys would say. She saw the little tremble of Nat's lips as she smoothed his hair, and her keen eyes grew softer, but she only drew the shabby figure nearer and said, laughing,—"I am Mother Bhaer, that gentleman is Father Bhaer, and these are the two little Bhaers.—Come here, boys, and see Nat."

The three wrestlers obeyed at once; and the stout man, with a chubby child on each shoulder, came up to welcome the new boy. Rob and Teddy merely grinned at him, but Mr. Bhaer shook hands, and pointing to a low chair near the fire, said, in a cordial[10] voice,—"There is a place all ready for thee, my son; sit down and dry thy wet feet at once."

"Wet? so they are! My dear, off with your shoes this minute, and I'll have some dry things ready for you in a jiffy," cried Mrs. Bhaer, bustling about so energetically, that Nat found himself in the cozy little chair, with dry socks and warm slippers on his feet, before he would have had time to say Jack Robinson. He said "Thank you, ma'am," instead; and said it so gratefully, that Mrs. Bhaer's eyes grew soft again, and she said something merry, because she felt so tender, which was a way she had.

"Now I am going to toast you well, and try to get rid of that ugly cough. How long have you had it, dear?" asked Mrs. Bhaer, as she rummaged in her big basket for a strip of flannel.

"All winter. I got cold, and it wouldn't get better, somehow."

---

[10] **cordial**—*warm and sincere*

"Robin, my man, trot up to Nursey, and tell her to give thee the cough-bottle and the liniment," said Mr. Bhaer.

Nat looked a little anxious at the preparations, but forgot his fears, in a hearty laugh, when Mrs. Bhaer whispered to him, with a droll look,—"Hear my mischievous Teddy try to cough. The syrup I'm going to give you has honey in it; and he wants some."

Little Ted was red in the face with his exertions by the time the bottle came, and was allowed to suck the spoon, after Nat had manfully taken a dose, and had the bit of flannel put about his throat.

These first steps toward a cure were hardly completed, when a great bell rang, and a loud tramping through the hall announced supper. Bashful Nat quaked at the thought of meeting many strange boys, but

Mrs. Bhaer held out her hand to him, and Rob said, patronizingly,[11] "Don't be 'fraid; I'll take care of you."

A Very Special Talent

Twelve boys, six on a side, stood behind their chairs, prancing with impatience to begin, while the tall flute-playing youth was trying to curb their ardor.[12] But no one sat down, until Mrs. Bhaer was in her place behind the teapot, with Teddy on her left, and Nat on her right.

"This is our new boy, Nat Blake. After supper you can say, How do you do? Gently, boys, gently."

As she spoke every one stared at Nat, and then whisked into their seats, trying to be orderly, and failing utterly. The Bhaers did their best to have the lads behave well at meal times, and generally succeeded pretty well, for their rules were few and sensible, and the boys, knowing that they tried to make things easy and happy, did their best to obey. But there *are* times when hungry boys cannot be repressed without real cruelty, and Saturday evening, after a half-holiday, was one of those times.

"Dear little souls, do let them have one day in which they can howl and racket and frolic, to their hearts' content. A holiday isn't a holiday, without plenty of freedom and fun; and they shall have full swing once a week," Mrs. Bhaer used to say, when prim people wondered why banister-sliding, pillow-fights, and all manner of jovial games were allowed under the once decorous[13] roof of Plumfield.

Nat found himself very well off behind the tall pitchers, with Tommy Bangs just around the corner, and

---

[11] **patronizingly**—*in a manner of superiority*
[12] **ardor**—*enthusiasm*
[13] **decorous**—*mannerly*

Mrs. Bhaer close by, to fill up plate and mug as fast as he could empty them.

"Who is that boy next to the girl down at the other end?" whispered Nat to his young neighbor under cover of a general laugh.

"That's Demi Brooke. Mr. Bhaer is his uncle."

"What an interesting name!"

"His real name is John, but they call him Demi-John, because his father is John too. That's a joke, don't you see?" said Tommy, kindly explaining. Nat did not see, but politely smiled, and asked, with interest,—"Isn't he a very nice boy?"

"I bet you he is; knows lots and reads like any thing."

"Who is the big one next to him?"

"Oh, that's Stuffy Cole. His name is George, but we call him Stuffy 'cause he eats so much. The little fellow next to Father Bhaer is his boy Rob, and then there's big Franz his nephew; he teaches some, and kind of sees to us."

"He plays the flute, doesn't he?" asked Nat as Tommy rendered himself speechless by putting a whole baked apple into his mouth at one blow.

Tommy nodded, and said, sooner than one would have imagined possible under the circumstances, "Oh, doesn't he, though? and we do gymnastics to music. I like a drum myself, and mean to learn as soon as ever I can."

"I like a fiddle best; I can play one too," said Nat, getting confidential on this attractive subject.

"Can you?" and Tommy stared over the rim of his mug with round eyes, full of interest. "Mr. Bhaer's got an old fiddle, and he'll let you play on it if you want to."

"Could I? Oh, I would like it ever so much. You see I used to go around fiddling with my father, and another man, until he died."

"Wasn't that fun?" cried Tommy, much impressed.

"No, it was horrid; so cold in winter, and hot in summer. And I got tired; and they were cross sometimes; and I didn't have enough to eat." Nat paused to take a generous bite of gingerbread, as if to assure himself that the hard times were over; and then he added regretfully,—"But I did love my little fiddle, and I miss it. Nicolo took it away when father died, and wouldn't have me any longer, 'cause I was sick."

"You'll belong to the band if you play good. See if you don't."

"Do you have a band here?" And Nat's eyes sparkled.

"Guess we do; a jolly band, all boys; and they have concerts and things. You just see what happens tomorrow night."

After this pleasantly exciting remark, Tommy returned to his supper, and Nat sank into a blissful reverie[14] over his full plate.

Mrs. Bhaer had heard all they said, while apparently absorbed in filling mugs, and overseeing little Ted, who was so sleepy that he put his spoon in his eye, nodded like a rosy poppy, and finally fell fast asleep, with his cheek pillowed on a soft bun. Mrs. Bhaer had put Nat next to Tommy, because that boy had a frank and social way with him, very pleasant to shy persons. Nat felt this, and had made several small confidences during supper, which gave Mrs. Bhaer the key to the new boy's character, better than if she had talked to him herself.

---

[14] **reverie**—*daydream*

In the letter which Mr. Laurence had sent with Nat, he had said—

Dear Jo,

Here is a case after your own heart. This poor lad is an orphan now, sick and friendless. He has been a street-musician; and I found him in a cellar, mourning for his dead father, and his lost violin. I think there is something in him, and have a fancy that between us we may give this little man a lift. You cure his overtasked body, Fritz help his neglected mind, and when he is ready I'll see if he is a genius or only a boy with a talent which may earn his bread for him. Give him a trial, for the sake of your own boy,

"Teddy"

"Of course we will!" cried Mrs. Bhaer, as she read the letter; and when she saw Nat, she felt at once that whether he was a genius or not, here was a lonely, sick boy, who needed just what she loved to give, a home, and motherly care. But she and Mr. Bhaer observed him quietly; and in spite of ragged clothes, awkward manners, and a dirty face, they saw much about Nat that pleased them. He was a thin, pale boy, of twelve, with blue eyes, and a good forehead under the rough, neglected hair; an anxious, scared face, at times, as if he expected hard times; and a sensitive mouth, that trembled when a kind glance fell on him; while a gentle speech called up a look of gratitude, very sweet to see. "Bless the poor dear, he shall fiddle all day long if he likes," said Mrs. Bhaer to herself, as she saw the eager, happy expression on his face when Tommy talked of the band.

So, after supper, when the lads flocked into the school-room for more "high jinks,"[15] Mrs. Bhaer appeared with a violin in her hand, and after a word with her husband, went to Nat, who sat in a corner watching the scene with intense interest.

"Now, my lad, give us a little tune. We want a violin in our band, and I think you will do it nicely."

There was a great clatter in the room, but as if deaf to any sounds but those he made, Nat played softly to himself, forgetting every thing in his delight. It was only a simple spiritual, such as street-musicians play, but it caught the ears of the boys at once, and silenced them, until they stood listening with surprise and pleasure. Gradually they came nearer and nearer, and Mr. Bhaer came up to watch the boy; for, as if he was in his element[16] now, Nat played away and never minded any one, while his eyes shone, his cheeks reddened, and his thin fingers flew, as he hugged the old fiddle and made it speak to all their hearts the language that he loved.

"You shall be first fiddle in my band," added Franz, with an approving smile.

Mrs. Bhaer whispered to her husband—"Teddy is right: there's something in the child." And Mr. Bhaer nodded his head emphatically, as he clapped Nat on

[15] **high jinks**—*loud, playful activity*
[16] **in his element**—*doing what he does best or enjoys most*

the shoulder, saying, heartily—"You play well, my son. Come now and play something which we can sing."

It was the proudest, happiest minute of the poor boy's life when he was led to the place of honor by the piano, and the lads gathered around, never heeding his poor clothes, but eying him respectfully, and waiting eagerly to hear him play again.

They chose a song he knew; and after one or two false starts they got going, and violin, flute, and piano led a chorus of boyish voices that made the old roof ring again. It was too much for Nat, more feeble than he knew; and as the final shout died away, his face began to work, he dropped the fiddle, and turning to the wall, sobbed like a little child.

"My dear, what is it?" asked Mrs. Bhaer, who had been singing with all her might, and trying to keep little Rob from beating time with his boots.

"You are all so kind—and it's so beautiful—I can't help it," sobbed Nat, coughing until he was breathless.

"Come with me, dear; you must go to bed and rest; you are worn out, and this is too noisy a place for you," whispered Mrs. Bhaer; and took him away to her own parlor, where she let him cry himself quiet.

After a while she won him over and as he told her all his troubles, she listened to the little story with tears in her own eyes, though it was not a new one to her.

"My child, you *have* got a father and a mother now, and this is home. Don't think of those sad times any more, but get well and happy; and be sure you shall never suffer again, if we can help it. This place is made for all sorts of boys to have a good time in, and to learn how to help themselves and be useful men."

If you enjoyed this excerpt from *Little Men*, you will want to find out more about the ten boys who make Plumfield their home. A third book, *Jo's Boys*, completes the story and tells how the boys grew to adulthood.

Time to Think

1. Who is the main character?
2. What was Plumfield?
3. What was Nat's talent?
4. How did Nat feel about being at Plumfield?
5. What made Plumfield a wonderful place?

In the Spotlight

Character Analysis

1. Classify these characters as either one-dimensional or multidimensional. Give a reason for your choices.

   Nat—________________________________

   Jo Bhaer—________________________________

   Tommy Bangs—________________________________

   Mr. Bhaer—________________________________

   Demi—________________________________

2. Which of the one-dimensional characters do you think have the greatest possibility to grow and develop further?

How can we help others overcome challenges?

In the late 1800s, some children were forced by circumstances to care for themselves. Boys like Nat who were directed to a home like Plumfield were fortunate. The boarding school offered a loving home and an education that would prepare orphaned or abandoned children for a successful adult life. When Nat knocked on the door, he was sickly and homeless with little hope. After arriving at the welcoming home, his hopelessness began to be transformed. Simple acts of kindness can transform feelings of dread into feelings of hope and peace. Today, children whose circumstances require the care of someone other than family are often placed in loving foster homes. This form of kindness continues to be a reflection of God's love. Proverbs 19:17 says, "He that hath pity upon the poor lendeth unto the LORD; and that which he hath given will He pay him again." God honors those who help children in need.

Compassion

James A. Sanaker

Compassion is love, plus desire to share
The trouble and tears that come from despair;
Compassion is love, plus sympathy, too,
With a will to help, to heal and renew.

Compassion is love, plus pity enough
To walk with the weary when the going is rough;
Compassion is love, plus the spirit to do
For others, our Lord had compassion, do you?

Time to Think

1. How does the poet use repetition?

2. In what ways can you be compassionate toward others? Answer by completing the acrostic using the letters in the word *compassion*.

C aring for those who are suffering
O ffering to listen to them about their needs
M ______________________________
P ______________________________
A ______________________________
S howing sympathy and support
S aying a kind word
I ______________________________
O ffering a helping hand
N ______________________________

Think on These Things

"Be ye all of one mind, having compassion one of another." —1 Peter 3:8

JOUST ◆ TOURNY

The Case of the Perplexed Playwright

Siera Weber

Lucas Miller, the lead—and only—detective of Miller's Mystery Management Agency has a new case to solve. Juan, the older brother of Lucas's friend Marcos, needs his help. Juan has written a play to be performed at the town's Renaissance Faire, but props and costumes keep disappearing. So far, this mystery remains unsolved. However, Lucas is now on the job, and he is determined that the play must go on!

Chattering voices and melodic instruments blended together in a symphony of sound as Lucas Miller wound his way through the booths of the annual Bakersville Renaissance Faire. His eyes studied the flurry of movement and color as he passed people in Renaissance-themed costumes—men in fancy doublets[1] and lacy ruffs, women in billowing dresses and embroidered coifs.[2] From a distance, he could hear the "knights" preparing for the upcoming jousting[3] tournament. The smell of horses, goats, and other live animals mingled with the scent of food floating from the different vendors. As Lucas traveled through "Ye Olde Craftsmen Corner," he admired the beautiful wares[4] at each table: blown glass, hand-tooled leather, pottery, hand-sewn clothing, metalwork, jewelry. He made a mental note to return there after he finished his mission.

[1] **doublet**—*a close-fitting jacket worn by men during the Renaissance*
[2] **coif**—*close-fitting cap*
[3] **jousting**—*combat between two knights using lances while on horseback*
[4] **wares**—*manufactured items for sale*

For even on a Saturday—even at the Bakersville Renaissance Faire—Lucas Miller could not rest. Just that morning, the lead (and only) detective of Miller's Mystery Management Agency had received a text from Juan, the older brother of his best friend Marcos. The message read:

If you can come early, stop by stage. Have problem.

So, although Lucas had planned to come to the fair only to watch Juan's play, he arrived early. To match the fair's theme, he wore a charming green doublet, brown trousers, and a fancy collar called a ruff. But on his head he wore his deerstalker cap, and on his feet he wore his sleuthing sneakers, ready to solve whatever mystery he might find.

Faint jingling and heavy footfalls thundered into Lucas's reverie. He turned his head just in time to see a figure in a gray cloak plow into him. Lucas and the figure went sprawling onto the dirt, both losing their hats.

"Why don't you watch where you're going?" the figure sputtered, scrambling to stand.

Raising his head slightly, Lucas squinted. Sighing, he stood and dusted himself off. "You were the one running, Theo."

Theo Briggins rolled his eyes. He scooped something off the ground and then pulled his cloak tightly around him, glaring at Lucas.

Shaking his head, Lucas turned and looked for his hat. It lay in the dirt next to a fiery orange-and-red jester's cap with three golden bells on the points. Lucas picked up both hats and held out the jester's cap to Theo. "Interesting costume choice."

Theo snatched the cap away. "Looks better than yours." He shoved it on his head with one hand, careful to keep his cloak closed with the other. "Besides, it wasn't my idea. It's for Juan's play."

Lucas raised his eyebrows. "You're in the play?"

"Yeah." Theo shrugged. "It's no big deal."

"I didn't know you liked acting."

"It's all right." Theo shifted from one foot to the other. "Basketball is way better."

Lucas nodded slowly, studying Theo. Theo's eyes flitted from Lucas to the surrounding booths, fingers twisting his cloak. After a moment, he muttered, "I've gotta go," and shoved past Lucas.

With a bemused[5] sigh, Lucas set his deerstalker cap firmly on his head and resumed his trek to the stage that lay in front of an old barn at the end of the fairgrounds. The actors and stage crew used the barn to prepare themselves and the props for each scene.

Using a side entrance, Lucas entered the barn and nearly collided with a couple of crew members wheeling a cannon through. Stepping out of their way, Lucas scanned the crowd for any sign of Juan or Marcos.

"I like your hat."

Lucas looked down to see a tiny girl staring at him with her bright green eyes. She wore a light-brown jerkin[6] and a brown muffin cap with blonde pigtails poking out underneath. She looked about four years old.

"Thanks. Who are you?"

---

[5] **bemused**—*bewildered; confused*

[6] **jerkin**—*a close-fitting hip-length sleeveless jacket*

"I'm Sophie."

"Are you in the play?"

The little girl held out a russet leather satchel. "I'm the courier."

"Important job." Lucas knelt down to Sophie's level. "I have a message for you to deliver. Could you tell Juan that Lucas Miller is here?"

"Do you have paper?"

"Um . . ." Lucas dug around in his pockets but couldn't produce paper or a pencil.

Sophie shrugged. "That's okay." She hugged her satchel to herself and ran away. In just a moment, she returned. "What's your name?"

"Lucas."

Sophie turned and ran back, weaving through the actors and stage crew milling about the big barn. Soon, she returned with Juan and Marcos in tow.

"Hey, Detective," Juan said with a tired smile. "I'm glad you're here."

"What's the problem?" Lucas asked.

"Mrs. MacIntosh is sick today, so I'm in charge of the entire production."

"Makes sense. It's your play, after all."

Juan laughed. "Yes, but I have a problem. Things keep disappearing."

Lucas looked around the barn. "A lot of people are moving a lot of things. Could just be an accident."

"I don't think so," Marcos interrupted. "All of the missing things are Rory's."

"Yeah," Juan nodded. "Where is he?" Juan scanned the crowd for Rory and waved him over. "He's playing Lord Justin, the main character."

As Rory made his way to the group, Lucas noticed that he had a sword belt but no sword, no ruff to go with his doublet, and no hat for his head—even though a nobleman in Juan's play would need a hat. *That is a little strange,* Lucas thought. *Rory doesn't usually lose things.*

"Hey, Lucas," Rory said. His eyes were a little red.

"You okay?" asked Lucas.

"Yep." Rory wiped his nose. "My allergies are just bugging me."

"That's the other weird thing," Juan interjected. "We've been rehearsing in this old barn all week, but Rory's allergies didn't kick in until today."

As if on cue, Rory let out a huge sneeze.

"What are you allergic to?" Lucas asked.

"Hay. And some animals, like goats. I can't go near the petting zoo." Rory sniffed loudly. "But I've been staying away from that side of the fair."

Marcos leaned over and picked something off the front of Lucas's doublet. "Did you stop by the stables, Lucas? You have some hay on your jacket."

Surprised, Lucas looked down at himself. *Where did that come from?* he wondered, backing away from Rory and brushing himself off.

"Anyway, some key pieces of Rory's costume are missing," Juan said. "A few people saw a suspicious person hanging around the dressing room area. If someone is purposefully stealing Rory's things, I want to know who and why."

"Sure thing." Lucas whipped out his magnifying glass.

"Great! Sylvie is already out looking for clues."

Lucas paused at the mention of his rival, Sylvie of Smith's Sleuthing Services. *Juan had asked her for help first?*

Noticing his friend's expression, Marcos quickly explained, "She's playing Lady Matilda. She was already here when we noticed the missing things."

Juan added, "I figured two detectives are better than one. The play is in an hour."

Lucas nodded. "I'm on it." He headed for the door.

"I'll go with you," Marcos offered.

Lucas paused. "Don't you need to rehearse?"

"Nah, I'm just stage crew."

"Oh." *That's weird,* Lucas thought. *He's been really excited about this play. He probably has the whole script memorized.*

"Can I come?" Sophie asked.

"Go ask your mom," Marcos said.

Sophie ran to a tall lady directing the stage crew as they moved props. Sophie tugged on the woman's arm and asked for permission. The woman nodded, and Sophie ran back and slipped her hand into Marcos's. "Mom said to stick with you."

"Okay." As Marcos, Lucas, and Sophie left the barn, Marcos explained, "Sophie is our neighbor. My mom babysits her sometimes."

“No, she watches me,” Sophie said. “I’m not a baby.”

Marcos smiled. “Watches.”

Lucas perused[7] the area outside the barn. “Where did the suspicious person go?”

Marcos pointed toward the jousting arena. “Sylvie went that way to look for him.”

As the trio tramped toward the jousting arena, Lucas asked Marcos, “Why aren’t you in the play?”

Marcos reddened slightly. “Juan wanted me to try out for Lord Justin, but—” he scratched his neck. “I hate being in front of people.”

“But you’re so good at memorizing!”

“Yeah, but—” Marcos shuddered. “I just—I can’t do it. Don’t you remember when we had to do oral book reports?”

Oh, right, Lucas thought. *That had not gone well for Marcos. He finished the three-minute report in forty-five seconds—and he forgot most of his points. Not to mention he was shaking for the rest of the class period.*

“Besides,” Marcos added, “everyone wanted to be Lord Justin. Even Theo auditioned for that role!”

What? Lucas thought. *He acted like the play wasn’t a big deal.*

As they neared the jousting arena, Sophie squealed, “Sylvie!”

Sylvie Smith sat dejectedly on a bale of hay outside the stables, her dress puffing out around her like a lilac-colored cloud. Her face was so pale it nearly matched the elaborate ruffled collar engulfing her neck. Lucas had never seen his rival looking so disturbed.

“You okay, Sylvie?” Marcos asked in alarm.

---

[7] **perused**—*read or examined carefully*

"Y—yeah." She cleared her throat. "I—um—I asked around, and some of the knights said they saw someone in a cloak sneak into the stables."

"Did you find any clues?" Lucas asked.

"I tried to." Sylvie lowered her head.

"What's wrong?"

"I—" A horse's loud neigh interrupted Sylvie's statement. She jerked in alarm, eyes widening.

Lucas raised his eyebrows in surprise. *Sylvie Smith—afraid of horses?* His rival always seemed so confident! An unfamiliar sense of sympathy stirred inside him. "Marcos and I can go look," he offered. "How about you babysit Sophie?"

"I'm not a baby!" Sophie stomped her foot.

"I know you're not," Sylvie said, "but would you mind sitting with me?"

Glaring at Lucas, Sophie climbed onto the hay bale beside Sylvie.

Curious horses stuck their noses outside their pens as the boys wandered through the stable, digging through the hay for clues. Finally, near the back exit, Lucas spied something white tucked behind a trough. "Look!" he exclaimed, holding it out for Marcos. It was Rory's lost ruff.

"Great!" Marcos exclaimed. "One down!"

"Guys!" Sylvie called, her voice wavering slightly as she stuck her head in the exit near them. "Sophie and I found this on the ground." She held out a little golden bell.

Lucas held his magnifying glass over it. "Interesting." He looked at his rival. "Good catch."

"Thanks," Sylvie smiled. Then a horse snorted, and she quickly backed out into the sunshine.

As the boys followed her outside, Lucas noticed a set of tracks pressed into the damp earth. He stooped down with his magnifying glass, following them from the stable to the nearby petting zoo. A few hurried workers rushed around, calling, "Butterscotch! Butterscotch!"

"What's going on?" Lucas asked a worker.

"Somebody opened our goat pen!" she sighed, exasperated. "We're missing one of our goats."

"Did you see who opened the pen?" Sylvie asked, pink notebook at the ready.

"I couldn't tell. Some guy in a cloak."

As Sylvie scribbled that down, Lucas narrowed his eyes. *Why was this mysterious stranger wreaking havoc all over the fair?*

As Sylvie looked up from her notebook, a shiny glint caught her eye. "Lucas! Look at that."

Lucas looked where she was pointing. A little golden bell lay in the grass next to the goat pen. Realization hit him. "Sylvie, can I borrow a piece of paper?"

Sylvie handed him her notebook. Lucas scribbled out a note, tore out the paper, and placed the paper and the bells in Sophie's satchel. "When we get back to the barn, take your bag straight to Juan. The rest of us are going to go catch a goat."

Perplexed, Lucas's friends and the petting zoo worker followed him as he hurried back to the stage. As soon as they entered the barn, Sophie took her satchel to Juan. Lucas led Marcos and Sylvie to the dressing room area, where Rory had climbed onto a table to get away from a little brown goat that was running around, bleating. Poor Rory's eyes and nose were running like a waterfall.

"How'd that—get—*achoo*—in here?" he exclaimed.

Lucas started to rush for Butterscotch, but the petting zoo worker grabbed his sleeve. "Hold on, don't scare her," she whispered. She reached into her pocket and held out a crumbled oatmeal cookie. "She loves these." The worker knelt down and coaxed the little goat toward her. Suspicious, Butterscotch sniffed at the worker's hand. After nibbling at

the cookie, she allowed the worker to lead her out of the dressing room area.

"You okay, Rory?" Marcos asked.

Three huge sneezes racked Rory's body before he could reply. "I don't think so," he sniffed. "I don't feel good, and I can't quit—*achoo*—sneezing. I think I need to go home." He wiped his nose. "Theo can take over."

"Theo?" Lucas asked.

"He's the understudy,"[8] Marcos explained.

"I see. Well, that solves the last piece of the puzzle!" Lucas exclaimed.

As Rory gathered his things to go home, the investigators headed backstage. Sure enough, Theo was practicing his lines as Lord Justin, now wearing a striking crimson costume and feathered hat instead of his pied[9] jester's ensemble. A prop sword rested in his belt.

"Oh, I'm glad you found the sword, Theo!" Lucas exclaimed. "We've been looking for that."

Theo froze for a moment, arm still raised for his monologue.[10] "Uh—yeah," he said, lowering his arm. "I found it under some costumes."

"Did you?" Marcos asked, narrowing his eyes.

"I'm sure he did, Marcos," Lucas said. "Right around the time he stole Rory's hat and ruff. Probably the same time he was hiding hay in the dressing room area, right before he went to steal a goat from the petting zoo."

"What?" Theo's eyes widened as he shifted from side to side.

"You weren't honest with me earlier, Theo," Lucas went on. "You do like acting, only you wanted a

---

[8] **understudy**—*a performer who studies and prepares to replace another actor if necessary*

[9] **pied**—*patchy or splotchy in color*

[10] **monologue**—*a dramatic speech performed by a single actor*

different role. You wanted to be Lord Justin. When they made you the jester and an understudy, you wanted to make sure Rory couldn't perform. You took hay from the stables to set off Rory's allergies. When that wasn't strong enough, you took drastic measures—stealing his costume and sneaking a goat from the petting zoo."

"You're crazy. That hat is getting to your head, Detective," Theo sputtered.

"Hey, Theo," Juan called. He strode toward the group with Sophie beside him. In his hands he held Lucas's note and the two bells. "Could I take a look at your jester's cap?"

Theo's face paled. "My cap?" he asked. "I—I'm not sure where it is."

"I don't think that's true." Juan frowned in disappointment. "While you're at it, why don't you bring me your gray cloak from Scene 4?"

Face flushing, Theo hung his head. "All right." He trudged to the dressing room, returning with a hay-covered cloak and his jester's cap. Only one tiny bell hung from the cap. The other two were missing.

"I'm disappointed in you, Theo," Juan said. "I'm afraid I can't let you participate. You need to go change, and then you need to go to the petting zoo and explain what you did."

"Okay. I'm sorry." Dejected, Theo shuffled away.

"This is just great," Juan sighed, rubbing his head. "Now I've lost my Lord Justin and my jester. Mike is the jester's understudy, but he's sick."

A cloud of disappointment hung over the group. Suddenly, Lucas brightened. "How many lines does the jester have?"

Juan shrugged. "Not many. He's just the comic relief. He follows Lord Justin around and makes jokes."

"So—the jester could maybe read his lines, as long as he makes them sound funny?"

Juan cocked his head to the side, considering. "I guess so. Yeah, why not? He could be a struggling jester who's trying to improve his routine."

"Great!" Lucas whipped off his deerstalker and plopped the jester's cap on his head. "I'll be your jester."

"That's really nice of you, Lucas, but without Lord Justin, we don't have much of a play. And he doesn't have an excuse to read off his lines."

"No problem," Lucas said confidently. "I know someone who has every word of this play memorized."

All eyes turned to Marcos, whose face paled. "I—I don't know."

"You don't need to," Juan reassured him.

"Well—" Marcos hesitated, grappling with his desire to help his brother and his fear of the stage.

Lucas laid a hand on Marcos's shoulder. "You won't be by yourself. I'll be up there with you the whole time."

Marcos looked at his friend, then at his brother. Finally, he cleared his throat and straightened his shoulders. "Well, the show must go on," he said.

Juan clapped his brother on the back. "Thank you, Marcos. I owe you for this."

"I want a turkey drumstick and three apple fritters after this," Marcos announced.

"Deal."

Juan's play was a great success. The audience loved the bumbling jester who struggled to remember his jokes, and they cheered for the brave feats of Lord Justin. Lord Justin did stumble over some of his lines, and his face remained pale for the first half of the play. But any time he was nervous, he glanced at the jester, who performed a cartwheel or tried to juggle as Lord Justin composed himself.

After the play, Sylvie approached Lucas. "You did a good job solving the mystery!"

"Thanks." Lucas hesitated, then added, "I wouldn't have solved it without those bells, though."

Sylvie smiled. "Sometimes two heads are better than one."

Lucas nodded. "Yes, they are."

Time to Think

1. Why was Lucas Miller at the Renaissance Faire?
2. Who was to play the part of the jester originally?
3. What was Sophie's role in the narrative?
4. Why did Juan conclude that it was no accident that things were missing?
5. Why was it odd that there was hay on Lucas's doublet?
6. Why was Rory so determined to stay away from the goat?
7. When Rory announced that Theo would have to take over his role in the play, Lucas said that was the last piece of the puzzle, meaning he had solved the mystery. Looking back, what clues that had previously perplexed Lucas now made sense?

In the Spotlight

Mystery

Which of the following elements of a mystery can you find in "The Case of the Perplexed Playwright"? Summarize your answers under each category below.

Mystery

- Main Character
- Problem or Puzzle
- Clues and Distractions
- Culprit

an excerpt from

The Quest for Seven Castles

book two in The Terrestria Chronicles
by Ed Dunlop

The main character, Josiah, was a captive, enslaved to the evil Argamor. He was rescued by King Emmanuel of Terrestria, who made him a son and a prince. Since that time, Josiah has lived in the Castle of Faith. He has learned many lessons from Sir Faithful, the steward of the castle. Today, however, King Emmanuel has summoned Josiah to leave the castle at once and set forth on a quest. He must go alone, but he has the book and the dove to guide him along the Path of Righteousness to the Castle of Virtue. Along the way, Josiah meets a friendly stranger, who offers to show him a shortcut to the castle. Josiah hesitates for only a moment before he takes the shortcut and finds himself entering the Village of the Littlekins.

As Josiah entered the Village of the Littlekins he stopped and stared around in astonishment. Both sides of the narrow street were lined with tiny cottages that were barely higher than his waist! He knelt in the street and studied the strange little buildings. "Who lives in these tiny houses?" he wondered aloud. "They're so small—they must have been built for rabbits!"

Reaching out to touch one little house, he lifted a tiny latch and opened a little door barely fourteen inches high. He knelt down and peered in through the tiny doorway. A small fire blazed merrily in a miniature fireplace less than twelve inches wide, and a cooking pot the size of a teacup hung over the flames, bubbling and steaming and filling the tiny chamber with a delicious aroma. Tipping his head to one side, he studied the interior of the little house, noting with amazement the little bed in one corner, the tiny benches, and the little table too small to hold a single roast goose.

Whoever lives here is hardly as tall as a chicken, Josiah told himself. *I've never seen such a tiny house! Perhaps these little houses were built for rabbits, or squirrels, or raccoons or badgers . . . no, raccoons and badgers would be too large to live here.* It appeared that the occupants of the tiny cottage were not at home, so he quietly closed the little door.

Still on his hands and knees, Josiah opened the door of the next little house and peered in. A piercing scream issued from within the little dwelling. Startled, he quickly closed the little door. He shook his head in astonishment. In the brief instant that he had looked inside the little house, he had seen two women down on their knees at a washtub filled with suds, vigorously scrubbing homespun garments. But the women were hardly as big as three-week-old-kittens!

He leaned close and tried to peer in the tiny window, hoping for another glimpse of the little women. However, the sunlight reflected off the glass and all he

could see was his own reflection. But he did hear more screams from inside the cottage.

Afraid that he had upset the mistress of the little house, Josiah turned and hurried back the way he had come until he was safely out of the strange little village. He saw a small stream by the side of the road, so he hurried down to it to refill his flask and take a drink. After he had refreshed himself he sat down on a fallen log on the creek bank to think matters through. He had seen no one in the strange little village—except for the unbelievably tiny women that he had frightened by peeking in the little door—but he felt uneasy just passing through.

The candlemaker said that this was the best route, he told himself. *If the Littlekins are all as small as those two tiny women are, what is there to be afraid of?* But he still couldn't dismiss the uneasy feeling inside. He couldn't explain it, but something inside told him that he was in great danger. He took a deep breath. *I'll just get to my feet and walk right through that tiny village!* he decided. *What can happen?*

"A thousand pardons,[1] my lord," a tiny voice said, interrupting his thoughts, "but would you be so kind as to allow me to take a seat on this log?"

Josiah stared, hardly able to believe his eyes. Standing before him was a tiny little imp of a man dressed in a green jerkin and brown leggings. The little man was slightly less than a foot tall, with spindly legs and arms and a curly, brown beard. "Who are you?" the young prince gasped in astonishment. "Where did you come from?"

"My name is Envy," the wee little man said, scratching at his beard with fingers hardly bigger than grains of rice. "I'm from the village."

"The Village of the Littlekins?"

The little man nodded proudly. "Aye."

"Then you must be a Littlekin," Josiah ventured, still trying to recover from the surprise of seeing a third adult too small to even reach his knee.

"Indeed, I am, my lord," Envy replied. He gestured toward the log with a tiny hand. "May I?"

"Certainly," Josiah responded. The man's name sounded ominous, and he had a certain crafty look about him, but he was such a little fellow that Josiah could not see how he could possibly do any harm. Envy took a flying leap, grasped the top of the log, and pulled himself up on top.

The little man had hardly settled himself on the log beside Josiah when another little man about the same size appeared. The newcomer was dressed much as the

---

[1] **pardon**—*forgiveness granted for a lack of courtesy*

first, except that his jerkin was pale blue. "My lord, this is a friend of mine," Envy said, eyeing Josiah carefully. "His name is Greed. Would you mind greatly if he were to rest on the log for a spell?"

"Aye, there's plenty of room," Josiah replied, studying the two little men with curiosity. Greed quickly made himself comfortable on the log.

Scarcely a minute had passed when Josiah looked over to see a third tiny man hiking through the underbrush and heading straight for the log. "Who are you?" Josiah asked. "I suppose that you would want a seat on the log, too."

"My name is Discontent," the tiny man replied. "If it's no trouble, my lord, indeed I would like to rest a bit." He was dressed in solid brown, and had a thin face and dark, beady eyes, which gave him a striking resemblance to a rat. Discontent clambered up onto the log and took a seat beside the first two tiny men.

Ten minutes later, the log was crowded. Twelve tiny men, not one of whom was tall enough to reach to Josiah's knee, were seated on the log beside the young prince. Josiah studied the group of Littlekins. For the most part they were dirty and rough and uncouth,[2] with gruff countenances and surly manners, quite different from the polite civility of the first visitor, Envy. They argued with one another, pushing and shoving and knocking each other off the log and in general becoming quite obnoxious. Their language was atrocious,[3] and Josiah began to feel very uncomfortable, even to the point that he began to wish that he had not allowed Envy to take a seat on the log in the first place.

---

[2] **uncouth**—*bad-mannered*

[3] **atrocious**—*extremely wicked, cruel, brutal*

Josiah noticed that from time to time the little men whispered to each other and eyed him as though they were plotting mischief against him. He felt no fear, since the men were so much smaller than he. *They probably don't weigh more than two or three pounds apiece,* he told himself.

"Hey, big one, make a little more room," a foul smelling little man named Idleness[4] growled at Josiah.

The young prince tried to scoot over just a trifle, but the Littlekin on the other side of him let out a squeal of rage. "Clumsy ox! Watch what you are doing! Keep to yourself! You have nearly squashed me!" He beat against Josiah's leg with his tiny fists.

"I beg your pardon," Josiah muttered, reminding himself that he had taken a seat on the log before any of these tiny men and wondering if he should bring the matter up.

"You are taking entirely too much room," a plump Littlekin named Gluttony[5] declared a moment later, glaring accusingly at Josiah.

"We will have to ask you to get down," another added.

Josiah laughed. "I was here first. It's my log. You are sitting here at my permission."

Josiah's words provoked a chorus of angry muttering. The Littlekins became violently angry and actually began to attempt to push Josiah off the log! The boy laughed as he pushed back. "You cannot hurt me," he taunted. "You are but a swarm of grasshoppers!"

One of the little men leaped to his feet and blew a long blast on a hunting horn. The sound reverberated[6]

---

[4] **idleness**—*laziness*

[5] **gluttony**—*excessive eating and drinking*

[6] **reverberated**—*continued to echo or resound*

through the trees. Suddenly becoming aware of the clamor of angry voices, Josiah turned to see a horde[7] of tiny townspeople rushing through the woods straight toward him. The men were carrying pitchforks, shovels, hayrakes and hoes; the women had rolling pins, brooms and other assorted weapons, and it was obvious that the furious inhabitants of the little town meant to do him harm. "It's one of the big 'uns!" a man's voice shouted. "Get 'im!"

Josiah leaped to his feet, but he was not alarmed in the least. The biggest man in the crowd was barely twelve inches tall. The angry horde of Littlekins swarmed around Josiah's ankles, stabbing and striking at his feet and lower legs with their tiny makeshift weapons. Josiah laughed. The little people were attacking him in fury, but their assaults felt like pinpricks. *With one good kick I could send thirty of them flying*, he told himself in amusement.

"Little folk, what are you doing?" he cried, doing his best to hold back his laughter at the absurdity of the assault. To him, the attack of the little people seemed as frivolous as a pack of mice attacking a lion. "I'm not your enemy!"

The angry horde swelled in numbers until the clearing was filled with tiny villagers. Shouting and screaming in their tiny voices, they surged forward, competing with each other for the opportunity to take a swing at the amused young prince. But their furious assault was having little effect; Josiah could hardly feel their feeble blows. "Kill him!" the Littlekins screamed to each other. "Envy, kill him! Discontent, chop his toes off! Laziness, slice his ankles to ribbons!"

---

[7] **horde**—*a large group, multitude; a crowd*

Josiah took a step backwards, stumbling over some of the little people and knocking them flat, though he managed to avoid stepping on any of them. The tiny villagers responded in a blind rage, swarming forward like a colony of oversized ants and screaming in their eagerness to do him harm. Swinging their tiny weapons, they battered his knees, shins and ankles with all their might. Josiah was doubled over with laughter at the absurdity of the situation. The attack of the Littlekins was having little effect upon him, but a good many of their furious blows were falling on each other, with telling results.

One brave young villager had ventured to scramble up into a thin sapling. He launched himself at Josiah, managed to catch hold of Josiah's belt, and hung on for dear life. Josiah brushed his tiny attacker away, doing his best not to hurt the little man.

"I am not your enemy!" the young prince called again, trying to reason with the horde of angry little people. "I'm just passing through on my way to the Castle of Virtue. Please stop! I do not wish to harm any of you."

But his words fell on deaf ears. The angry mob of Littlekins now numbered in the hundreds. They surged forward, shouting and swinging and pressing against his shins until he was compelled to take several steps backwards. Suddenly his boots caught and he found himself falling backwards. Two of the Littlekins had strung a rope between two trees and managed to trip him. As he hit the ground, the mob shouted exultantly and swarmed over him like ants on a dead grasshopper.

Prince Josiah still was not alarmed as he rolled over and leaped to his feet. If it was a fight that these Littlekins wanted, then it was a fight they were going to get! But somehow the frantic hordes of tiny villagers had managed to throw a rope around him, and, as he attempted to stand up, they jerked him down into the dust again. Josiah lunged upward against the tiny rope, flinging dozens of little people to the ground like so many toy dolls. He struggled to his knees, but the Littlekins pulled him to the ground again by the sheer weight of their numbers.

"Get off me!" Josiah shouted, struggling and thrashing about in a desperate attempt to free himself.

"Let go of me!" He threw his arms wide, scattering Littlekins left and right. He grasped the rope about him and attempted to pull it off. The Littlekins swarmed over him again, shouting and kicking and hitting him.

Realizing for the first time the seriousness of the situation that he was in, Josiah pulled the book from his doublet and swung it mightily. In an instant the little black volume became a two-edged sword. The Littlekins leaped back in fright as the glittering blade sliced through the air. Josiah advanced slowly, swinging the sword with all his might. The tiny villagers retreated before him, squealing with fright as they scattered like autumn leaves before a gust of wind. He gave a tremendous sigh of relief when he saw how easily the Littlekins could be put to flight.

At that moment a heavy weight came crashing down on the back of his head. Josiah saw a brilliant flash of white light explode inside his head. The sword fell from his hand. Darkness descended abruptly.

Prince Josiah awoke to find that he was lying in the shade of a giant oak. When he tried to move he discovered that his hands were tightly bound behind him. The Littlekins were swarming about him, dancing up and down in delight as they celebrated their capture of such a large prisoner.

Josiah rolled over and attempted to struggle to his feet, but the rope brought him crashing to the ground. The Littlekins had him firmly under their control.

The crowd of Littlekins abruptly parted. A small company of soldiers came dashing up with tiny swords drawn, stopping just inches from Josiah's face. Smartly dressed in red doublets with gold braid, white leggings, and shiny black boots, the pint-size soldiers were under the command of a stern-faced officer by the name of Captain Temptation. "On your feet, prisoner!" the captain roared, holding the point of his tiny sword against the tip of Josiah's nose. "On your feet, before I run you through!"

The young prince rolled over and struggled to his knees. Though his hands were bound behind him, he glanced around desperately for his sword. He caught a glimpse of three red-uniformed troops struggling under the weight of the weapon as they carried it through the trees. "Come back with that!" Josiah shouted. His heart sank. Without the sword he was helpless—even against his tiny captors—and he knew it.

"On your feet, prisoner!" Captain Temptation ordered again. Josiah sighed and grudgingly obeyed.

The villagers had formed a double line, each with a firm grip on the long rope, and now they began to pull him toward the village. Tiny as they were, their combined weight and strength was too much for the young prince, and he was forced to follow meekly along. *They caught me off guard,* Josiah berated[8] himself. *If I had been alert and watchful, this would never have happened. It all started when I allowed Envy to take a place beside me on the log.*

He looked down at the tiny captain who was marching proudly alongside his prisoner. "Where are you taking me?"

"You must stand before our magistrate,[9] Lord Careless," Captain Temptation replied, "to answer the charges against you."

[8] **berated**—*scolded or rebuked; criticized*

[9] **magistrate**—*an official responsible for the administration of the law*

"What charges?" Josiah demanded.

"You will find out when Lord Careless deals with you," the tiny soldier answered, giving Josiah a disgusted look. "Now move along quietly."

The triumphant Littlekins proudly paraded their prisoner through the narrow streets of their tiny village, laughing and chattering as they marched along. Josiah shuffled through the lanes with his head down, overwhelmed at the suddenness of his capture. *I have failed again*, he thought bitterly. *I have failed King Emmanuel! But the Littlekins are so tiny. Who would have thought that there were so many of them, or that they could fight so efficiently?* Remorse filled his soul. *I should never have allowed Envy to take a place on the log, even though he is so tiny. Once again, I have failed my King! I should never have listened to the candlemaker and detoured through the village of the Littlekins!*

The procession reached the center of the village and approached a large building with stately pillars and marble steps. Josiah stared at the massive building which seemed so out of place among the tiny dwellings. As the Littlekins led him up the steps, a growing sense of dread overwhelmed him. *So this is the Courthouse—the place where I will stand before Lord Careless.*

Once inside the building, the Littlekins abandoned their places on the rope and scattered to find seats, leaving Josiah in the charge of Captain Temptation and his company of tiny soldiers. Even though there were only ten or twelve of the pint-size troops and Josiah could easily have overpowered several times that many, he was too discouraged and defeated to even try to resist. Meekly he allowed himself to be led to the front of the crowded courtroom.

A tiny, gray-haired bailiff[10] with a large, droopy mustache stood upon a raised platform at the front of the courtroom. "Court is now in session," he cried in the loudest voice he could muster, "with the Honorable Lord Careless presiding. All rise!"

The throng of noisy Littlekins jumped to their feet and a hush fell over the room. A dignified Littlekin wearing a long black robe entered through a side door. Upon his head was a powdered wig. Even before the magistrate walked to the raised desk in the center of the platform, Josiah knew that the robed figure was the Honorable Lord Careless.

"Be seated," Lord Careless said in a flat, toneless voice. "Defendant, approach the bench."

Josiah was standing directly in front of the platform—so close that he could have reached out and touched the desk—so he merely raised his eyes and looked at Lord Careless.

"The defendant will approach the bench!" Lord Careless declared loudly. His voice was still flat and lifeless, but his eyes flashed with anger. Josiah inched half a step closer. "That's better," the magistrate declared. "By what name are you called?

"Prince Josiah of the Castle of Faith, Your Honor."

The magistrate unrolled a parchment and studied it in silence for half a minute. Then he leaned over and looked down at Josiah. "Does the defendant understand these charges against him?"

"Your Honor, I have not even heard the charges," the young prince replied. "What are they?"

"Do you understand the charges against you?" Lord Careless demanded sharply. Usually it is quite difficult

---

[10] **bailiff**—*an officer that has the responsibility to maintain order in a courtroom*

to speak sharply in a monotone, but the tiny magistrate managed it quite nicely.

"Sire, what are the charges?" Josiah asked again.

"Just answer the question," the magistrate snapped irritably, as though he was already tired of the affair, though the court had just been called into session.

"Nay, sire, I do not understand the charges," Josiah asserted, "for I have not yet heard them. And I don't understand why your people have arrested me, for I was merely planning to pass through your village without harming—"

"Silence!" Lord Careless roared, a remarkable feat for a man his size. He snatched the parchment from his desk and thrust it at the bailiff. "Read the charges."

"Aye, my lord." The bailiff held the document up in front of his face and began to read. "The people of the Village versus the giant stranger, Prince Josiah. The prince is charged with trespassing, entering our village with malicious[11] intent to harm, creating a disturbance, malicious assault, maligning[12] the citizenry, inciting a riot, and resisting arrest." He rolled the parchment up and handed it back to Lord Careless.

[11] **malicious**—*spiteful; willfully harmful*
[12] **maligning**—*speaking harmful, untrue words*

"That's ridiculous!" Josiah protested. "I didn't do any of those things!"

The frightened young prince looked around the courtroom in desperation, for there was no question that Lord Careless and the tiny inhabitants of the Village of the Littlekins had determined evil against him. He looked beseechingly[13] to the back of the courtroom at Envy, the Littlekin who had first approached him so politely, but the little man glared back as maliciously as the rest of the villagers. Josiah realized that there was nothing he could do—his hands were securely bound and the rope was still around him. He was at the mercy of the court.

"Stand and be sentenced!" Lord Careless ordered. Josiah was already standing, but he knew now that the tiny magistrate expected a response, so he simply leaned closer to the bench. His head slumped in defeat.

"Your malicious crimes against the citizenry of this village are numerous and of great magnitude. I hereby sentence you"—Lord Careless paused and Josiah winced[14]—"to a duel between you and any male citizen of your choosing."

"A duel?" Josiah's head shot up. "What kind of a duel?"

"A test of strength," the magistrate replied. "A contest of force. You are to engage in a wrestling match. If you shall win, you shall go free. But if you lose, you are our slave forever."

"But, sire, I am not guilty!" Josiah protested.

"Select your opponent."

"I am to choose, Your Honor?"

"Select any male citizen of this village," the magistrate repeated slowly, as if irritated at Josiah's dullness. "You

---

13 **beseechingly**—*with urgent pleading; imploringly*

14 **winced**—*flinched; shrunk back*

will wrestle him. If you can prevail, you are free; but if you shall lose, you are our slave forever."

An expectant hush fell over the crowd as Josiah gazed around the courtroom. *I can whip any ten of these puny little men,* Josiah thought scornfully. *I can whip twenty, or thirty! Lord Careless must not realize just whom he is dealing with here.* His gaze fell upon Envy. *He's the one responsible for this whole predicament,*[15] Josiah thought angrily. *I'll squash him like a bug! His arms are about as thick as my little finger!*

He turned to face Lord Careless. "I choose Envy."

"Envy?" The magistrate addressed the tiny man. "Do you accept the challenge?"

Envy stood to his feet. "With pleasure, Your Honor."

"Unbind the defendant," Lord Careless ordered, and Captain Temptation stepped forward to carry out the order. Josiah knelt so that the tiny soldier could reach the ropes. In no time, his hands were free and the ropes were removed.

He stood to his feet and watched Envy as he strode confidently forward. A leering[16] grin was on his tiny face, and he flexed his skinny arms, almost as if he expected to win the match. Josiah shook his head in disbelief. *I'm more than five times as tall as he is! I weigh fifty times as much as he does! Doesn't this little fellow realize what he is up against?*

Josiah began to relax. *This won't be so difficult after all. Once I beat this skinny little runt, I'll leave the Village of the Littlekins behind me and continue with my journey to the Castle of Virtue. I can't lose against such a puny adversary.*

---

[15] **predicament**—*a difficult, perplexing, unpleasant situation*

[16] **leering**—*sly, malicious*

As the grinning Littlekin marched toward the front of the courtroom to accept the challenge, Josiah's mouth dropped open. He stared in dismay. With each step he took, Envy was growing a little larger. He was halfway down the aisle and already he was nearly five feet tall. By the time he reached the front of the room, the tiny Littlekin had become a hulking giant of a man, more than eight feet tall, with huge arms and shoulders that bulged with powerful muscles!

Seizing the terrified prince by the throat, the enormous Littlekin lifted him off the floor with one hand.

"I accept the challenge, Your Honor," he growled in a deep voice that reverberated like thunder throughout the courtroom. "Aye, I look forward to it!" He relaxed his grip and allowed the boy to sink to the floor.

Overcome with fear, Josiah rose slowly to his feet. If he lost the match against his gigantic adversary, he was to be the slave of the Littlekins forever. He trembled at the thought.

"The match will now begin," Lord Careless announced. "Envy, loyal resident of our village, will combat the defendant, Prince Josiah, of the Castle of Faith. If the defendant wins the match he will be acquitted[17] of the charges against him. If Envy wins the match, the defendant becomes our slave forever."

Eager to fight the young prince, Envy leaned forward with a cruel leer on his features. Josiah's heart pounded with fear. Just moments before the Littlekin had been a tiny man less than a foot tall, but now he was well over nine feet. The crowded courtroom was filled with the chants of the excited villagers. "Envy! Envy! Envy!"

Prince Josiah was desperate. He quickly scanned the courtroom, frantically seeking a way out of his dilemma, but the exits were blocked with throngs of Littlekins eager to witness the duel. He glanced back at Envy. His hulking adversary was growing faster and faster and was now more than ten feet tall! Completely overcome with terror, Josiah backed away.

The huge Littlekin grinned smugly as he took a menacing step forward. "Come to me, Prince Josiah of the Castle of Faith," he taunted, beckoning with his thick, hairy hands. "I shall show you a thing or two!"

---

[17] **acquitted**—*found or declared not guilty of a crime*

"King Emmanuel, I desperately need your help," Josiah whispered. Fear swept over him in waves and his chest felt so tight that he could scarcely breathe. His trembling legs seemed ready to give way at any moment. *A petition! I must send a petition to His Majesty!* Lacking a parchment to write upon, the young prince snatched the rolled document from the hands of the startled bailiff. *I don't have time to put my petition into words,* he thought frantically. *I just hope that King Emmanuel will understand my unspoken plea!*

"A petition to my King," he said softly, holding the rolled parchment aloft. He released it, and to his relief, the petition shot from his hand and vanished from the courtroom.

"What manner of craftiness is this?" Lord Careless demanded, leaning across the bench and glaring at Josiah. A murmur of angry Littlekin voices swept across the crowded courtroom. Captain Temptation and his red-uniformed troops drew their swords and started forward.

"Use your sword," a still, small voice prompted, and in the midst of his confusion and terror, Josiah heard. He looked up. The dove was perched on the chandelier directly over the magistrate's bench. "Use your sword. His Majesty's power is found within your sword."

Josiah nodded. What was it that Sir Faithful had said when speaking of the dove? *"Obedience to his voice will guarantee success in your quest for the seven castles."* The sword! Where was it?

The royal sword lay across the desk within reach of Lord Careless. Josiah leaped to the platform, seized the weapon, and whirled about to confront Envy. He sprang directly at the gigantic Littlekin, swinging the invincible weapon with all his might. The suddenness of the move caught Envy by surprise, and he leaped back to evade the blade. Encouraged, the young prince charged forward, swinging the sword furiously.

Cowed[18] by the threat of the glittering sword, Envy retreated, stumbling backward over the masses of Littlekins huddled behind him. He struggled to regain his balance and then tumbled to the courtroom floor with a resounding crash as the terrified Littlekins leaped in all directions to avoid being crushed by the enormous bulk. Shrieks of outrage filled the courtroom.

Quick to follow through with his momentary advantage, Josiah whirled and dashed to the door at the opposite side of the courtroom. Littlekins blocked the way, but Josiah's sword sliced left and right with lightning swiftness. With shrieks of terror the tiny villagers scattered like chaff[19] before the wind. Captain Temptation and his tiny soldiers were nowhere in sight. Josiah dashed through the door, slamming it behind him.

"Follow me!" a small voice called, and the young prince turned in time to see the dove dart into the shadows of the forest behind the courthouse. Josiah plunged into the dense woods and ran as hard as he could.

He caught a glimpse of the dove's beautiful white plumage and dashed in that direction. Following the flight of the dove, he soon came to a moss-covered cabin. An elderly man stood before the cabin door as if waiting for him. "Come in hither, my prince," the man called as Josiah came in sight. "You shall be safe with

[18] **cowed**—*intimidated, frightened by threats*
[19] **chaff**—*grain husks that are separated from the seed during threshing*

me!" The dove darted into the cabin, so Josiah felt that it was safe to follow. The man stepped in behind him and closed the door.

"I must hide!" Josiah blurted, breathing hard. "The Littlekins will soon be here!"

The old man turned slowly. His face was calm and peaceful and his clear gray eyes sparkled with friendliness. "The Little Sins will not venture to pursue you, Prince Josiah," he replied softly. "They fear the power of your sword."

Josiah stared at the old man. "Little Sins?" he echoed. "But sire, they are called the 'Littlekins.' I saw it on the sign at the entrance to their village!"

"Little Sins," the cabin owner corrected gently. "You have misread the sign." He shook his grizzled[20] head sadly. "Many a child of the King has been caught off guard by the Little Sins, as you were today. Envy, Gluttony, Pride, Apathy,[21] Greed—they all seem so small and so harmless, but once they are allowed to abide in the human heart, they quickly take over. The Little Sins are often just as deadly adversaries as the transgressions[22] that we would consider the 'Big Sins.'"

Josiah nodded and held his sword against his side. When it changed into the book, he thrust it carefully inside his doublet. "They nearly conquered me," he said in agreement. "They wanted to make me a slave forever." He paused and looked at the old man in bewilderment. "Sire, how did you know my name?"

"I am a nobleman in the service of King Emmanuel. My name is Sir Wisdom. I was sent here to help you

---

[20] **grizzled**—*having partly gray hair*
[21] **apathy**—*lack of interest or concern*
[22] **transgressions**—*violations of laws or commands*

on your journey to the Castle of Virtue. As you have learned already, there will be many obstacles for you to overcome before you can reach the castle."

Although Prince Josiah has escaped this time from the Little Sins, he has not reached even the first of the seven castles he is to visit on his quest. Sir Wisdom has reminded him that he has two precious guides—the book and the dove—that will never lead him astray. The road that Josiah must take is long, and he must ever be alert to the traps that Argamor has set along the way. To take your journey alongside Prince Josiah, you will want to read the full account in *The Quest for Seven Castles*, the second book in The Terrestria Chronicles, by Ed Dunlop.

In the Spotlight

Figurative Language

The Quest for Seven Castles is an **allegory** that uses symbolism to explain deeper truths. Characters, objects, and places represent other concepts, things, or ideas. The story itself can be enjoyed as it is, but there is a second meaning within the story that is deeper and more important. Match each symbol to what it represents to understand the deeper meaning in the story.

Castle of Virtue •	• God
Dove •	• Prayer
King Emmanuel •	• Little Sins
Littlekins •	• Word of God
Path of Righteousness •	• Holy Spirit
Petition •	• the first step in becoming more like Christ
Sword •	• Obedience to God

I WONDER . . .

1. How did Josiah arrive at the village of the Littlekins?
2. Describe the Littlekins.
3. After the Littlekins captured Josiah, he was sentenced to wrestle one of them. Why did Josiah choose to wrestle with Envy?
4. Do you agree with Josiah's reasoning? Why or why not?
5. As Envy approached Josiah, he grew until he was enormous. What was the author symbolizing here?
6. What did Josiah finally remember to do when he needed help?
7. How did Josiah defeat the Littlekins? Explain the symbolism behind the circumstance.
8. Who was the wise man that the dove led Josiah to, and why was he there?

What is our purpose?

Have you ever begun cleaning your room and gotten distracted? Perhaps you picked up your phone and began texting a friend or playing games and lost track of the time. When we are given a specific purpose or task to complete, we need to finish to the best of our ability. Distractions always make a task last longer than necessary. Josiah allowed the Littlekins, or Little Sins, to distract him from the path that led to the Castle of Virtue—a place of becoming more like Christ. At first, the Littlekins seemed harmless; however, when they joined forces, they became too hard for Josiah to defeat.

When Josiah finally remembered the purpose of his trip, he refocused on the final goal. Proverbs 3:5–6 reminds us to "Trust in the LORD with all thine heart; and lean not unto thine own understanding. In all thy ways acknowledge Him, and He shall direct thy paths." When our purpose is to obediently follow God and reflect His likeness, He will help us to avoid the distractions that can lead us in a wrong direction.

The Unfailing One

Phillips Brooks

The little sharp vexations,[1]
And the briars that catch and fret,[2]
Why not take all to the Helper
Who has never failed us yet?
Tell Him about the heartaches,
And tell Him the longings, too;
Tell Him the baffled[3] purpose,
When we scarce know what to do.
Then, leaving all our weakness
With the One divinely strong,
Forget that we bore the burden,
And carry away the song.

[1] **vexations**—*irritations; annoyances*
[2] **fret**—*to cause worry and irritation*
[3] **baffled**—*extremely confused and puzzled*

Think on These Things

1. Do the "briars that catch and fret" compare to large or small troubles? Explain your answer.
2. Who is the Helper and why is the poet encouraging the reader to take the little things to Him?
3. What do you think the poet means by "carry away the song"?

If Only I Had a Green Nose

Max Lucado

"It's the latest thing!" "Everyone has it." "You won't really fit in unless you have one too." "You are missing out!"

Sound familiar? Looking like everyone else—whether it's the brand of shoes you wear or the way you fix your hair—seems to be very important to many people. The latest thing in the village of the Wemmicks is to have a green nose. Punchinello knows that, like all Wemmicks, he is created one-of-a-kind by the master craftsman, Eli. But everyone is getting a green nose. It's Willy Withit's latest fashion statement. If Punchinello doesn't get his nose painted green today, he could miss out on this new trend!

Lucia and Punchinello looked out the window of Eli's workshop. Like other Wemmicks, they were wooden people. But unlike the other Wemmicks, they weren't standing in line in the village below.

"Look at them all!" Punchinello exclaimed.

"I don't understand it," Lucia wondered. "Why would anyone want to paint his nose green?"

"Because everyone else is," Eli responded without looking up from his workbench.

Punchinello didn't understand. "What do you mean?"

"Everyone wants to look like everyone else. Sometimes it's square hats. Sometimes it's tall shoes. Why, last year the big thing was yellow ears. Now it's green noses. Everyone wants a green nose."

"Does a green nose make them smarter?" Punchinello asked.

"No."

"Does a green nose make them stronger?"

"No."

"Does it make them faster?"

"No."

"Then what does a green nose make them?"

Eli looked up and smiled. "Greener."

But his smile left as he looked out the window at the long line of Wemmicks. "They think they'll be happier if they look like everyone else. But I made them different on purpose. Freckles, long noses, bright eyes, dark eyes . . . these were my ideas. Now they all want to look the same."

"Not me," said Lucia. "I'm happy just the way you made me."

"Me too," agreed Punchinello. "I don't need a green nose to feel special." Then he paused and looked at the village. "But I would like to see how a green nose looks up close. Want to go?"

Eli smiled as the two stood to leave.

"Just remember, I made you different on purpose," he told them.

From street level the line looked even longer and the noses even greener. Lucia and Punchinello worked their way to the front of the crowd and watched as one Wemmick after another stepped into the nose-coloring store and came out painted.

"It's the latest thing," barked a Wemmick on the sidewalk. "Don't be the only Wemmick with a plain nose."

"Who is that?" asked Punchinello.

Lucia shrugged. "I don't know."

"Why, that's Mr. Willy Withit," volunteered a Wemmick from behind them.

"Does he run the nose-painting store?" asked Punchinello.

"More than that," the Wemmick explained. "Painted noses were his idea. So were the square hats and the tall shoes and the yellow ears. New things are his thing. He decides what is 'withit.' Isn't he the best?"

Lucia and Punchinello took a good look at this tall Wemmick with the deep voice, big smile, tall hat, and green bow tie that matched his oh-so-great green nose. Both were thinking the same question. Lucia asked it. "Who made him the new-thing picker?"

The Wemmick looked puzzled, like he'd never been asked that question. "Well, I don't know. He always has." Then his eyes brightened. "Wait, look, here comes a new nose!"

"Oooh," said the Wemmicks.

"Ahhh," admired some of the others.

The just-painted Wemmick didn't stop to speak—he just kept his nose in the air and walked past. All the green-nosed Wemmicks did this. After all, how could your nose be seen if it wasn't in the air?

Walking around high-nosed, however, was risky. Wemmicks walked into walls, doors, even each other. Lucia and Punchinello had to be very careful. One Wemmick took up the whole street.

"Step back, step back," he announced. It was the mayor. "Make way, every Wemmick. My wife is coming in for a touch-up." With one hand he waved back the citizens. With the other he guided her through the crowd.

"Horrible, just horrible," she cried, covering her nose with both hands. "I chipped some paint when I bumped into a tree. Now the real me is showing. Horrible, just horrible."

As the crowd passed, Lucia shook her head. "Such a fuss over a green nose."

"Yeah," agreed Punchinello. "You'll never catch me in the nose-coloring store."

"Aw, Punch, I was hoping you'd go."

Punchinello recognized the voice immediately. "Twiggy?" He turned and looked at the wide-eyed, sweet-smiling Wemmick. His ears began to turn red. They always did when he saw her. He reached up and covered them.

"Why don't you paint your nose, Punch? I painted mine. Everyone else is painting theirs. Besides, you'd look good in green." Twiggy reached up and touched the tip of his nose. "Yours is so cute." With that she turned and walked away. "Bye-bye." She waved.

Punchinello moved one hand from his ear to his nose. He turned and looked at his reflection in a store window.

Lucia had to grab his hand to get his attention. "Come on, Punchinello. Let's go."

As he walked past the store, he noticed Willy Withit examining his nose in a handheld mirror. Later at home, he did the same. "I never noticed before, but my nose sure looks pale."

The next morning, Punchinello walked down the street with his friends Splint and Woody.

"Are you really thinking about it?" Woody asked.

"Sort of," Punchinello answered.

"They say the paint stings your nose," Woody volunteered.

"And it stinks," Splint added.

"The brush could get in your eyes," Woody continued.

"And it only comes off with sandpaper." Splint nodded.

"Shhh." Punchinello put a finger to his lips

and pointed at a large crowd of green-nosed Wemmicks standing in the square. "Something's going on."

The mayor was standing on a platform. His wife (nose freshly painted) and Willy Withit were on either side of him. "Welcome, one and all, to the first meeting of the Nosey Wemmicks Club," he announced. "Your glistening green sets you apart as a 'Withit Wemmick.'" As if on cue, Wemmicks began stroking their noses. "You are classy. You are keen. You are awesome. You are green!"

Proud of his poetry, the mayor smiled, and the Wemmicks applauded. "We owe it all to Willy Withit," he shouted over the noise, "the pioneer of the painted snout!" Everyone applauded even louder.

"People love me because of you!" one shouted.

"I have more friends!" cried another.

"With a green nose, I am a better Wemmick!" exclaimed a third.

The mayor hung a medal around the neck of Willy Withit. "You have changed the face of Wemmicksville. We salute your brilliance. Without you we'd all look like . . ." The mayor paused, looking for the right word. Then he saw Punchinello and his friends. Pointing in their direction, he declared with a scornful laugh, ". . . them!"

Everyone else laughed too. Punchinello and his two friends lowered their heads and covered their noses.

"Let's hear it for Willy Withit," shouted the mayor, "the Wemmick who discovered the cure for the common nose!"

As the townspeople shouted and applauded, Woody, Splint, and Punchinello quickly turned and walked away.

They didn't stop until they stood in front of the nose-coloring shop. Within a matter of minutes all three were painted and walking down Wemmick Lane.

"Hey, Punchinello," asked Splint, pushing his nose upward, "am I doing it right?"

Punchinello didn't look, "I can't see you, Splint. If I turn, my nose won't be in the air."

"Whew, this is tough work," Woody added. "Not only do you have to get painted, but you have to walk weird."

"Yeah, but doesn't it feel great to be withit?" Punchinello asked.

And for a few days it did. They hung out with other green-noses and made weekly visits to the nose-a-curist for a nose-polish. They bought nose-gloves for cold days and nose-brellas for rainy ones. All three read Willy Withit's new book, *Winner by a Nose*. Most of all, they enjoyed looking down their noses at the unpainted Wemmicks.

"Step right up," shouted Willy Withit from the steps of his store. "Green noses are out, and red noses are in!"

"But we just got our noses painted green!" they told him.

"No problem," he replied. "Our red will cover the green. Step right up and get in style."

The three friends looked at each other sadly. "We thought we were in style," Woody moaned. What could they do but stand in line and have their noses painted red? For a few days they fitted in, until one morning they saw a blue-nosed Wemmick.

"Oh, no," they said to each other, "not again." So they changed colors.

But it was only a short time until blue noses were out, and pink noses were in.

Then pink was out, and yellow was in.

Then yellow was out, and orange was in.

Soon Punchinello and his buddies had so many layers of paint on their noses that they couldn't remember what they really looked like.

"This has to be the final color," they said the day they walked out with orange noses.

But once again they were wrong. "I'm so tired of this," Woody moaned when he saw a purple-painted Wemmick. "I wish my nose was common again."

The three sat on a rock and hung their heads. "Me, too," agreed Punchinello. "I should have listened to Eli."

"You think he would help us?"

"Why don't you ask him?"

All three turned at the sound of the familiar voice. "Lucia," they said.

"He asks about you every day," she told them.

"Is he mad?" Punchinello wondered.

"Sad, but not mad."

Punchinello looked up toward Eli's house on the hill.

"He told me to tell you to come." Lucia spoke again.

"Could I take my friends?"

"Of course."

"Would you go with me?"

"Certainly."

And so the four began the long walk up the hill to Eli's house. When they reached the top of the hill, Eli stepped out of the workshop and began walking toward them. He met them in the yard. One by one he examined their noses.

"Been trying to fit in, eh?"

Punchinello nodded.

"Did you succeed?"

"Not really. Every time we got close, someone changed the rules."

"That's the way it is."

"And my neck hurt from sticking my nose in the air," Woody added.

"You weren't built to walk that way."

"We just want to be ourselves again," Splint said.

"I'm glad to hear that."

"Can we?" they asked.

"Of course you can," Eli replied. "I'll always help you be who I made you to be." Then he reached in his pocket and pulled out a piece of sandpaper. "But it's going to take some time."

And so Punchinello and his friends followed their maker into his workshop where he spent the rest of the day removing the paint. It hurt to be sanded, but it was worth it to be normal again.

I WONDER . . .

1. What was the advantage to having a green nose?
2. After just a little time went by, what did Punchinello and his friends realize about trends and fads?
3. Why do you think Punchinello felt that having his nose sandpapered was worth it, even though it hurt?

In the Spotlight

Figurative Language

1. Which genre is represented in this selection? Explain your answer.
   a. allegory b. biography c. historical fiction
2. Who was behind the idea that every Wemmick needed a green nose and what is the significance of his name?
3. What do you think the Wemmicks' green noses symbolize?
4. Punchinello's friend Woody confessed that his neck hurt from sticking his nose in the air. Eli reminded him that he was not built to walk that way. As you think about the meaning of the idiom "with your nose in the air," what do you think Eli was really telling Punchinello and his friends?
5. What is the moral of the story?

Have you ever wished you were different?

Maybe you have wanted to be taller, smaller, brown eyed, blue eyed, or better at sports or math like your friends seem to be. Did you know that God made you exactly the way He wanted you to be to fulfill His purpose for your life?

Psalm 139:14 says, "I will praise Thee; for I am fearfully and wonderfully made: marvelous are Thy works; and that my soul knoweth right well." God made each part of creation beautiful in its own way and for a unique purpose. Trying to change ourselves to be like someone else often brings emptiness and dissatisfaction.

1 Samuel 16:7 tells us that God wants us to be more concerned about the condition of our hearts than our physical appearance. "But the LORD said unto Samuel, Look not on his countenance, or on the height of his stature; because I have refused him: for the LORD seeth not as man seeth; for man looketh on the outward appearance, but the LORD looketh on the heart." Who you are on the inside is much more important than what you look like on the outside. The Wemmicks forgot that and missed out on the joy of life and time with their maker as they tried to keep up with the trends. God's designs and plans are always perfect, and we can flourish knowing that we were created for great things!

Frozen Victory

Charles Coombs

At the mere sight of Bret or his unruly dog Spot, Jimmy can feel his temper rise. Why must they always show up just in time to spoil things for him? Well, Jimmy's not about to let them ruin his chance to win the most important race of the winter.

It was a cold, crisp day on Miller Pond. Jimmy Benton was right in the middle of cutting a smooth figure eight, when the black-and-white dog came barking and slipping across the ice. At the last moment, both Jimmy and the dog tried to dodge out of each other's way. But the ice was too slippery. The wildly pawing dog crashed into Jimmy just below the knees. Both of them wound up in a heap on the wet ice.

"Ki-yi-yi-yi—" The dog scrambled away, losing its footing every few steps.

"Ha-ha-ha."

Jimmy knew that laughter. Even before he turned, he felt the anger rising in him.

"Bret!" Jimmy got his skates under him and faced the husky, sandy-haired skater who was getting so much pleasure from the mishap. "How about keeping that mutt of yours off the pond? One of these days he's going to get hurt, and. . . ."

"Quit kidding," Bret laughed. "Spot can outskate you any day of the week. And he doesn't even have to wear skates to do it. Don't worry any about my dog. But you better start worrying about the big race tomorrow. I don't want to win it too easy, you know."

"You won't," Jimmy said hotly.

With Bret there, Spot had regained his courage. He kept just out of reach and yapped annoyingly at Jimmy.

Jimmy liked dogs. But Spot had been a constant source of trouble to him. First, he had chewed up the newspapers along Jimmy's route one morning. On another occasion he had run out from behind a hedge and knocked Jimmy off his bike. Spot had meant to be friendly, in his clumsy way. But that didn't mend the seven broken spokes,[1] or straighten out the bent forks of the bike.

And now, after his hard spill on the ice, Jimmy felt a soreness creep into his hip. With the big race coming up tomorrow, too!

Sometimes he wished that Bret's dog was a thousand miles away and still running. Oh, Spot was a good enough dog, Jimmy had to admit. But Bret just never had bothered to train him. He was always barking at people, jumping up on them, and making a general nuisance of himself.

---

[1] **spokes**—*rods that connect a wheel's hub to its rim*

It was Bret's fault, really. Any dog could be trained to behave itself if its owner would take the time and patience. Bret seemed to get a big kick out of Spot's pranks.

The next morning Jimmy rolled over in bed and was awakened by the soreness in his hip.

"It's just a bruise, son," his mother said of the black-and-blue patch of skin. "But perhaps it would be better if you didn't race today."

"But, Mom, I have to," Jimmy said quickly. "The winner at Willow Lake gets to race at the big Winter Festival next month. I . . . I'd rather race at the Winter Festival than be . . . well, be President."

"Well, since we already have a good President," his mother smiled, "I'll try not to stop you from racing."

"The soreness will go away, Mom," Jimmy said hopefully. "It's even getting better now. If it hadn't been for that annoying dog of Bret's. . . ." He left the sentence unfinished. Every time he thought of that dog it made his blood fairly boil.

It was another clear day at Willow Lake, but it was a little too warm for the best skating. The ice was slightly mushy and wet. There were a few rather thin spots. In fact, warning flags marked a couple of places farther out on the lake where the ice had broken.

Jimmy was lacing up his skates when he glanced up and saw Spot bounding in and out of the crowd. A quick chill went along Jimmy's spine. That dog was a jinx[2] for sure. As soon as he saw Jimmy, he set up a wild yapping.

Trying to ignore the dog, Jimmy kept right on lacing his skates. Suddenly he was showered with water and ice shavings, as Bret braked to a stop in front of him.

---

[2] **jinx**—*something that is thought to bring bad luck*

"Hey!" Jimmy spluttered, "what's the big idea? If you're looking for trouble, I'll . . ."

"Oh my," Bret mocked. "Were you sitting there, Jimmy? Here, let me brush you off."

"Just leave me alone," Jimmy bit out. Between Bret and his dog Spot, they sure had managed to make life miserable for him lately.

"I just wanted to warn you," the husky boy in the red-and-blue ski cap said. "Don't get in my way during the race. I'm counting on winning."

"Who isn't?" Jimmy said. "So am I!"

"You're just going to try," the bigger boy said. "I'm going to win."

"Phooey!" Jimmy stood up to test his skates. Spot lunged in, barking and nipping playfully at his ankles. It startled Jimmy. His skates went out from under him. Again he sat down hard on the wet ice.

Bret skated away, holding his sides laughing.

"You'd better tie that mutt up," Jimmy shouted after him. "Or there's going to be trouble!"

If Bret even heard, he didn't pay any attention.

The one-eighth-mile oval racing course was marked off with flags. The Junior Boys' race was to be a half mile—or four laps around the oval.

The ten young contestants crouched at the starting line. From the inside position, Bret grinned confidently over at Jimmy. "Don't forget," he called, "keep out of my way."

"Baloney!" Jimmy shot back. He found himself glancing around for Bret's dog. At least Spot didn't seem to be around. Maybe his paws had gotten too cold and he had decided to go back home. Jimmy hoped that was the case. He couldn't afford to have Bret's dog messing up his chances today.

The starter's gun cracked its sharp report across the wide expanse of ice that covered Willow Lake. The crowd that ringed the oval cheered as the ten skaters surged forward.

Bret sprinted ahead, taking an early lead. Then he eased off to a smooth distance-eating pace. Way back in sixth place, Jimmy knew that Bret would plan the race so that he would have plenty of strength left for a final sprint in the fourth lap.

Each time they hit a straightaway, Bret glanced back over his shoulder to see that no one was threatening his lead. When he needed to, he put on an added sprint.

By the end of the second lap Jimmy had moved up into third place, and was gaining a little on Bret with every yard. A feeling of confidence surged through him. His bruised hip barely bothered him now. His legs felt strong. Unless Bret was holding a lot of speed in reserve, Jimmy felt confident that he could catch him before the finish line was reached.

Then, as he glanced up for a moment, out of the corner of his eye Jimmy noticed a small dark object far out on the ice near the center of Willow Lake. In the brief flash of time that he saw it, before the view was screened out by the spectators lined around the oval, Jimmy realized that it was Bret's dog.

"Good thing," Jimmy thought happily. "At least, the troublesome little hound won't be ruining my chances to win the race."

Midway through the third lap, the skaters had spread out. With a sudden burst of speed in the near

straightaway, Jimmy surged ahead until he was in second place.

Only Bret was ahead of him. A scant ten yards ahead, at that. The larger boy's skates seemed slightly heavy on his feet. Jimmy figured that Bret had set too stiff a pace during the first half of the race, and was tiring fast.

Then, going into the final straightaway of the third lap, Jimmy caught another glance off across the ice as he skated past a gap in the ring of spectators.

And what he saw in that one quick glance nearly made him lose his balance.

Far out on the frozen lake, his head barely visible above the surface, Spot was pawing frantically at the jagged edge of the ice.

Beads of sweat broke out on Jimmy's forehead. That dumb hound, to let himself fall through a hole in the ice! Well, someone was bound to see him, or hear him yapping. Besides, a dog could keep his head above the water for quite a while. And he, Jimmy, had a race to win.

Trying to shake off the vision of the floundering dog from his mind, Jimmy turned on more speed. As they started on the final lap, he was almost up with Bret. Deep down he knew that he was going to beat Bret. His legs felt good, and it was easy to see that Bret was tiring.

"Oh boy," Jimmy thought happily, "Winter Festival here I come!"

Bret glanced back over his shoulder. There was a frightened look on his face. He seemed to realize that Jimmy had enough power left to overtake him before the lap was finished.

Then, at a time when he should have been putting every thought into passing Bret, Jimmy's eyes jerked sideways, as though pulled by some unseen power. Off across the lake he saw Spot still struggling. But more slowly. No one seemed to have seen or heard the dog. Everyone was so intent upon the race, and there was so much yelling, that no one was paying any attention to what might be taking place on other parts of Willow Lake.

"Bret," Jimmy yelled at the back of the boy ahead of him. "Spot! He fell through a hole, and. . . ."

But Bret merely attempted to put more speed into his skates. It was obvious to Jimmy, then, that Bret figured he was just trying to throw him off stride.

He was just swinging out wide to pass Bret when a sense of guilt surged over him, and Jimmy knew that, race or no race, there was only one thing that he could do.

At any moment a tired Spot might sink below the surface of the icy water. It was no time to be thinking about winning the race, or about how much trouble the dog had caused him.

The thing that mattered was that the dog's life was in peril—extreme peril.

As the people watched with mouths agape, Jimmy suddenly swerved off the racecourse, sped through an opening in the crowd, and sprinted straight off across the frozen lake.

All thoughts of winning the race were gone now from his mind. Jimmy's only hope was that he hadn't waited too long in realizing where his real duty lay. He only hoped that he would reach Spot in time.

It seemed forever by the time Jimmy covered the two hundred yards across the lake. Approaching the jagged hole in the ice, he went down on his stomach and inched toward the edge.

"Easy, Spot," he soothed. "I'll have you out of there in a jiffy."

The dog's pleading eyes stared wildly at him. Spot could barely keep his head above the water.

"Give me your paw, Spot," Jimmy panted, lying flat and reaching far out. "Attaboy. Right here, boy. Good dog, Spot."

The dog yapped and pawed a little more frantically on the rough edge of the ice. Then Jimmy caught hold of one of the dog's feet. Hopeful that the ice wouldn't give way beneath him, Jimmy heaved on the dog.

Then he got hold of his collar. With a hefty, yet careful tug, Jimmy pulled the dog out onto the ice. Sighing his relief, and trying to control the sudden shivering of his body, Jimmy slid quickly back from the hole and got to his feet.

Bret came streaking across the ice. Some of the race officials were close at his heels.

"Jimmy!" Bret gasped. "I thought you were just trying to pull a fancy one when you yelled at me about Spot. I thought you. . . ."

"Yeah, I know," Jimmy said. "And I don't blame you. I'd have figured the same thing."

"I . . . I don't deserve winning the race," Bret said.

"Sure you do," Jimmy replied with a smile. "It doesn't matter to me, Bret. But I'm sure glad that I didn't wait any longer before. . . . Well, I'm sure glad I got to Spot in time."

Jimmy knelt and snuggled the wet dog to him. Spot wagged his cold tail and licked Jimmy's hand. "He's a good dog, Bret," Jimmy laughed. "A real good dog."

He hadn't noticed that the race judges were huddled with their heads together over at one side. Then one of the judges walked over to him.

"Jimmy," he said, "everyone is agreed that this year Willow Lake can afford to enter two junior contestants in the Winter Festival. One for winning the race around the oval course; the other for winning a much more important race."

"Hurrah!" Bret cheered wildly.

". . . we, therefore, award to you, Bret, and to you, Jimmy, . . ."

But the judge's words were drowned out by the loud cheers of the crowd.

Bret and Jimmy pounded each other happily on the shoulders, while a wet and cold black-and-white dog bounded joyously from one to the other.

Think on These Things

While Jimmy's purpose at the beginning of the story was to win the race, the circumstances that came his way presented the higher purpose of putting another's need before his own desires. Winning a race is not a bad purpose. However, sometimes our purpose may need to shift when someone else's well-being becomes a needed focus. Romans 12:10 says, "Be kindly affectioned one to another with brotherly love; in honor preferring one another." Jimmy realized that his new purpose needed to be saving Spot. In the end, both Jimmy and Bret were awarded for winning the race, but Jimmy was the true winner.

Time to Think

1. Why did Jimmy dislike Bret's dog?
2. What was Jimmy's goal?
3. During the race, what did Jimmy see that made him lose his concentration?
4. What was the outcome of the race?

I WONDER . . .

1. Categorize each of the following events as rising action, climax, or falling action. Explain your answers.
   a. Jimmy noticed that Spot had fallen through the ice.
   b. Jimmy tried to warn Bret that Spot had fallen in, but Bret ignored him.
   c. Jimmy realized that the dog's life was in peril and that it was up to him to save Spot.
   d. Jimmy and Bret are both declared winners.
2. What did Jimmy's act of compassion reveal about Bret? What did it reveal about Jimmy?

In the Spotlight

Foreshadowing and Mood

1. Which of the following facts foreshadows the main event?
   a. Jimmy was annoyed by Bret's dog.
   b. Jimmy bruised his hip.
   c. The ice was mushy, wet, and thin in spots.
   d. Warning flags marked where the ice had broken.
   e. Jimmy noticed Spot in the crowd and felt uneasy.
2. How does the use of foreshadowing affect the mood of the story?

True Greatness

C. E. Flynn

A man is as great as the dreams he dreams,
As great as the love he bears,
As great as the values he redeems,
And the happiness he shares.

A man is as great as the thoughts he thinks,
As the worth he has attained,
As the fountains at which his spirit drinks,
And the insight he has gained.

A man is as great as the truth he speaks,
As great as the help he gives,
As great as the destiny he seeks,
As great as the life he lives.

In the Spotlight

Elements of Poetry

1. Which of the following are found in "True Greatness"? Explain your answers.
   alliteration **free verse** **repetition** **rhyme scheme** **stanza**
2. How does the poet effectively communicate the theme?

Defeating Distraction with Purpose

Proverbs 23:7 says, "For as he thinketh in his heart, so is he." We are what we think, love, and value. We become what we dream about and pursue. True greatness springs from the depths of godly character. It is made visible by the truth we speak and the love we show.

The Lipizzaners

The Lipizzaners[1] are possibly the oldest breed of horses in Europe. Their breed began in the 1500s, when the emperor of Austria decided to produce the ultimate warhorse. He established horse farms, imported famous Spanish warhorses called Andalusians, and combined them with a rugged local breed known as the Karst. Other horse breeds, carefully selected for their physical characteristics and temperament, were added to the program. Today, for a horse to be a true Lipizzaner, its heritage must trace back to one of six stallions that are considered the founders of the breed.

Although the Lipizzaners were bred to be warhorses, their physical characteristics and calm temperament make them excellent saddle horses, carriage horses, jumpers, and show horses. The Lipizzaner's average height is from 15.1 to 15.2 hands. The *hand*, which equals four inches, is the unit used to measure a horse's height. Since adult horses of all breeds range in height from 14 to 17 hands, the Lipizzaner is a relatively short breed. Lipizzaners weigh from 1,000 to 1,300 pounds. They have long heads and backs, muscular necks, and deep, wide chests. Many Lipizzaners have a

[1] **Lipizzaners** (lĭp′ĭt·sä′nərs)

"Roman nose"—a nose that has a slight outward curve. Although most Lipizzaners are gray, many turn white as they age. Because Lipizzaners are docile and sensitive, they respond quickly to praise or displeasure. They are also highly intelligent, focused, and trainable.

The Lipizzaners' traits make them excellent horses to master classical riding techniques at the Spanish Riding School. The school, located in Vienna, Austria, has been operating for 450 years. Its name reflects the Spanish ancestry of the Lipizzaners.

The Spanish Riding School teaches a difficult form of *dressage*. *Dressage* means "training" in French. In dressage, a horse performs a series of precise movements. The rider guides the horse through its performance by giving it cues—movements of the rider's hands, legs, or weight. The cues are so subtle that the audience can barely see them, but the horse recognizes them instantly.

Each horse begins training by learning the basic "groundwork." Groundwork includes all the maneuvers that are performed without leaving the ground. The stallion progresses to learn the "airs above the ground," maneuvers during which the horse leaves the ground. Even the best horses never learn all of these maneuvers. In a lifetime of training, most stallions learn only one or two of these "airs." The riders at the Spanish Riding School spend eight to ten years training with their stallions.

For centuries, the Lipizzaners of the Spanish Riding School performed only for the Austrian royal family and their guests. Since the end of World War I, performances have been open to the public. If you ever have a chance to see these magnificent horses in action, it is something you would not want to miss!

Glossary of Terms

canter — One of the horse's natural gaits. A canter is faster than a trot, but smoother and slower than a gallop.

capriole (kăp′rē·ōl) — The horse leaps upward but not forward, with its forelegs tucked in. At the height of its leap, the horse kicks its hind legs out straight behind it into the air. The horse then lands in the same spot from which it started.

courbette (kôr·bĕt′) — While balancing on its hind legs, the horse tucks in its forelegs and jumps forward on its hind legs a number of times before putting its forelegs back on the ground.

gait — A horse's particular way of moving. The four natural gaits are walk, trot, canter, and gallop. Each gait is characterized by the rhythm and the sequence in which a horse lifts its feet, as well as by its speed.

passage (pə·säzh′) — A slow, elevated, majestic trot. Each diagonal pair of feet is lifted and returned to the ground rhythmically, with an upward and forward movement.

capriole

courbette

piaffe (pyăf) — The horse does not move forward but appears to remain on the same spot while performing the high, slow, rhythmic steps of a trot.

pirouette (pĭr′o͞o·ĕt′) — While moving at a canter, the horse makes a complete turn using its hind legs to pivot.

quadrille (kwŏ·drĭl′) — An intricate set of choreographed movements, set to historic music from the early 1800s, is performed by a group of eight Lipizzaner stallions.

The following excerpt is from *White Stallion of Lipizza*, by award-winning author Marguerite Henry. Although this is a work of fiction, the setting and two of the characters, Colonel Podhajsky and Borina, are real; many of the events are based on a collection of true stories. The Lipizzaner stallions continue to perform the airs above the ground to spellbound audiences even today.

an excerpt from

White Stallion of Lipizza

Marguerite Henry

Twelve-year-old Hans Haupt dreams of becoming a riding master. He was enthralled with the Lipizzaner stallions he saw every morning, especially the magnificent lead horse Borina. But Hans is just the son of a baker, destined to become a baker himself. A series of events—some of which are tragic—brings huge changes to Hans's life. As this excerpt opens, Hans, now fifteen, is an apprentice at the Spanish Riding School. He has two "professors." One is Bereiter Wittek,[1] a Senior Riding Master with years of experience. The other is a four-legged professor, none other than Borina himself!

Week by week the work stepped up in pace. Alone, and in groups. With music, without music. From the walk, trot, canter he graduated to the intricacies of the pirouette. Borina played no tricks here; he threw himself into the movement with such gaiety and precision that Hans couldn't help catching the rhythm. Pivoting on his haunches, forelegs stepping high, Borina danced around his hind feet as if they were nailed to one spot. In a flash of remembering Hans saw the porcelain statues in the shop windows. He and Borina were molded

[1] **Bereiter Wittek** (bĕ·rī′tər vĭ′tĕk)—*horse trainer Wittek*

together . . . just like that. Except he and Borina were *alive*! Waltzing!

The days flowed together. The pirouette and the passage became habit. Muscles were doing the memory work. By daily repetition they acted intuitively, faster than thought. Less and less Hans carried on his dialog with his inner self. Yet the more proficient he became, the more impatient he was to go on. He had come to the Riding School to learn the mighty leaps above the ground.

Every night he studied them in the book of instruction which Fräulein[2] Morgen had loaned him for the tenth time. There was no falling asleep now; he was too near his goal. He studied the pen-and-ink drawings of the aerial maneuvers. Just by blinking Hans could bring them alive! In color! Then he closed the book and did the courbette in his mind. He was glad that this was Borina's specialty. The capriole with its movement of horizontal flight was spectacular, breathtaking; the horse appeared to do the splits in midair. But to a horseman like himself, the courbette was greater. Any powerfully built stallion who could do a succession of forward

---

[2] **Fräulein** (froi′līn)—*German word for "Miss"*

jumps, holding himself erect on his hind legs, and carrying a rider besides—well that was. . . . He sighed deeply, unable to think of a word big enough.

One night when Herr[3] Braun was putting the chessmen back into their box, Hans dropped his book, walked over and confronted him. "Sir!" he asked in exasperation. "When will I ever begin the airs above the ground?"

The Rider-Candidate showed surprise. "The work you are doing on the ground," he said, "is perhaps more difficult than the work above the ground. One leads to the other—but slowly. If you are so impatient," he added almost brusquely,[4] "you should return to your bakery."

Hans stood as though someone had struck him hard across the face. His mouth opened, but no sound came out. Becoming a full-fledged Riding Master was the only way he could see how he could live. Like a puppy who had been scolded, he went over to his end of the room. In silence he put his book away in his wardrobe. In silence he undressed and crawled between the covers. He stared fixedly at an invisible spot on the ceiling. For a moment he blamed the naked electric light bulb for the moisture in his eyes. He knuckled a tear away.

"Ach,[5] Hans," the voice of Herr Braun was more gentle now, "all good growth is slow growth. Like a tree. You still have much work ahead on the piaffe between the pillars." He spoke slowly, emphasizing each word. "You see, Hans, the piaffe is the first stage for all aerial work. It is like a base from which the rocket flies! Only a horse and rider who do it well can work together above the ground."

---

[3] **Herr** (hĕr)—*German word for "Mister"*
[4] **brusquely**—*gruffly*
[5] **ach** (äkh)—*German word meaning "oh!"*

“Thank you, sir,” Hans sighed, resigned to the truth. Always there seemed another year, another month, another movement, another step, another something before he got his chance.

The very next day Bereiter Wittek ordered Borina readied for the piaffe, wearing the padded noseband with rings attached. Had Herr Braun confided last evening’s conversation? Hans was too breathless to care, almost afraid to believe he was getting so near his goal.

“At last, Hans, we try you on the piaffe,” the Bereiter said. There was a hint of pleasure in his voice as he tied Borina between the posts. “This for you is a big step forward. Now then, Hans, do you know what the piaffe is?”

“Yes, sir. It is a prancing in place, with very short steps. It is a sort of . . .” Hans hesitated.

“Of what?”

“A sort of . . .” Hans was afraid to put it into words.

Herr Wittek clapped his hands in impatience.

“. . . a getting ready for the courbette,” Hans blurted out.

“Exactly! Now let’s see if you can do it.”

At first, sitting there proudly on Borina’s back, Hans’s heart flooded with energy, with the promise of the future. Borina lifted his legs like pistons and put them down again in the selfsame spot. Through every fiber of his being Hans could feel the lofty upward thrust. Up and up, never advancing, never backing.

Then, startled, Hans suddenly felt a strange lateral movement. He was bewildered. “Something’s wrong,” he told Bereiter Wittek.

Quickly the man untied Borina. “Trot him away. Very extended. Then come back to me.”

Hans did as he was told.

"Always after the piaffe," the Bereiter explained, "a stallion must have a relief from the muscle tension of the short, sustained steps."

"Yes, sir; I understand, sir. But what happened? I felt a change in Borina's action. He suddenly seemed to go sideways instead of up. What happened?"

The Riding Master's head nodded. He was smiling, like a father whose boy has earned his first merit badge. "Borina ignored your signals at the beginning," he said. "He did the piaffe without any real guidance. Then, he expected some help from you. You must have been giving strong aid on one side and weak on the other. Now, see if you can give even pressure with both legs."

After the third try, followed by the free-moving trot, Herr Wittek ordered Hans to dismount and reward Borina. "I must reward you, too, Hans. You quickly sensed the ugly lateral movement and corrected your error. To me this shows promise for your future."

Hans was too happy to reply.

Glowing with pride, he took the small leather pouch from his pocket and poured a mound of sugar onto the palm of his hand. Borina lipped it in slobberly fashion. As he ground and swallowed the juicy sweetness, he eyed Hans familiarly, as much as to say, "It's been quite a session, eh, boy?"

The following Saturday, like a flash of lightning Colonel Podhajsky[6] announced the news, looking directly at Hans: "One of our Riding Masters is taken seriously ill.

---

[6] **Colonel Podhajsky** (kûr′nəl pōd·hătch′skē)

Bereiter Wittek will ride his stallion in this week's performance, and we'll need you, Hans, to ride Borina."

"Me?" Hans asked with a quick catch of his breath. He looked into the dark eyes questioningly. Why, this was like skipping a year in school, almost like graduation!

The eyes smiled back. "You will take part in the last event only, the quadrille. Now then, at ten o'clock this morning we rehearse—to music. There will be the usual tourists and visitors in the galleries; so it will be like a regular performance. Be saddled and ready for your entrance at eleven."

Hans was terrified and thrilled all at the same time. He had never worked before an audience. The galleries had always been empty. Besides, the quadrille was the grand climax of the entire ballet.[7] Next to the aerial leaps, he thought it the most beautiful of all. For a year now he and the other young riders had been practicing the precise figures—the turns and movements on two tracks, the flying change of leg on the canter, half pirouettes, full pirouettes, the passage and, last of all, the piaffe. He knew them! He was ready!

He put on the cinnamon-brown frock coat and the bicorn hat belonging to some previous rider. "You'll have your own someday," the tailor told him. "That is," he added, clapping Hans on the back, "If you have better luck than the last fellow who wore this."

[7] **ballet** (bă·lā′)

Eleven o'clock came. In the anteroom[8] of the hall the eight riders silently mounted their snow-white stallions, and silently lined up. Then to the airy music of the Polonaise[9] they entered the great hall as at a performance. Colonel Podhajsky led the procession, followed by Bereiter Wittek, then Hans on Borina, then Herr Braun. Hans felt tremulous yet somehow secure between these two men who wanted him to succeed. Borina was serenity itself, his ears busy with the music, pulling in the familiar melody.

The music heightened the pleasure for Hans, too, as they paraded in stately fashion between the red-white-and-red flags that crowned the training pillars. Keeping his body erect, his shoulders parallel to Borina's, he felt in perfect harmony, felt himself ready for tomorrow's performance! Ready for anything! Even in the entrance-walk, the joy of rhythm, the pride in Borina filled him with such a fullness that he wondered if the buttons on his uniform might spew into the air. Of all the stallions Borina seemed most buoyant,[10] most obedient.

Up in the galleries the morning visitors were on hand. Hans had been carefully schooled to be oblivious of them. He tried to remember this as he sensed a movement in the first gallery. He was turning in a platoon[11] of four when his attention was caught by a blue beret[12] waving wildly. Out of the tail of his eye he saw the

---

[8] **anteroom**—*an outer waiting room that opens into another room*

[9] **Polonaise** (pŏl′ə·nāz′)—*a stately, marchlike Polish dance popular in the 19th century*

[10] **buoyant**—*light, energetic, cheerful, seeming to float*

[11] **platoon** (plə·to͞on′)—*a group of people doing something together*

[12] **beret** (bə·rā′)—*a round, soft, brimless cap that fits snugly and is often worn angled to one side*

figure of Jacques leaning far out over the railing. And sitting behind him, the boy's father, grinning.

In that hairbreadth of divided attention Hans unconsciously tightened his reins. Instantly Borina sank back on his haunches, raised up his body in the beginning of a courbette and dumped Hans onto the floor like a sack of potatoes. There was a soft thump as he hit.

The music did not stop. Nor did the complex pattern of the dance. Only Hans's heart stopped, then it bumped against his chest. He could feel the Colonel's glance like an icy finger. Overcome with misery Hans scrambled to his feet and caught up to Borina, who was setting one leg carefully across the other in cadenced[13] movement with the other horses. Remounting, he closed the space which Herr Braun had kept open. Over and above the violins, he could hear guffaws and giggles from the galleries, and the sound of a slapped thigh.

Later, back in the stables, Hans worked in a trance. He took off the handsome coat that didn't belong to him anyway. He rubbed Borina dry—under his saddle, along his chest, down his legs. The stallion submitted with pleasure, scratching his head against Hans's shoulder to relieve the itchy places where the bridle leathers had been. He still felt playful, and he nipped a piece of Hans's shirt without touching the flesh beneath.

In spite of his torn heart Hans neglected none of the routine. He took more pains, if anything, as if this were their last time together. "I don't blame you," he said, feeling the stallion's breath brushing against his cheek. "But what will I do now? How else can I live?" he asked, beseeching.[14]

The limpid[15] eyes held no answer. Only the boy's reflection in their purple-brown depths.

His grooming done, Hans closed the stall door behind him. He walked past the stablemaster, moved down the corridor, and up the worn stone steps to his room. It was empty. Carefully he hung his borrowed uniform

---

[13] **cadenced**—*marked by a rhythmical pattern*
[14] **beseeching**—*earnestly requesting*
[15] **limpid**—*clear, calm, and unworried*

in the wardrobe. He brushed the sawdust from the beautiful brown serge[16] and he buttoned up the silver buttons. Even third-hand, the uniform would still be almost as good as new. He put on an old shirt and a pair of work trousers, and pulled out his father's old brown satchel from under the bed. He packed in it the few clothes he had brought with him. They were too small now, but they would fit Jacques. As he snapped the lock, he heard a violent cough behind him and turned to see Kurt. With red-faced kindness the boy said, "Colonel Podhajsky is talking below with Bereiter Wittek. They want to see you."

"I know." Hans picked up his satchel. For a long while he stood in the doorway, glancing around the room in good-bye. He shook hands with Kurt. Then he squared his shoulders and went down the stairs.

The stable seemed deathly quiet. Herr Stallmeister, his assistant, the feed master, grooms, and stableboys all were going about their duties, silent and remote, like figures in a dream. Staring straight ahead, Hans took one heavy step forward, then another. He heard Colonel Podhajsky and Bereiter Wittek in low-voiced conference near Borina's stall. He moved toward them, toward what was going to happen to him. When he was within earshot, the talk ceased.

Time stood still. The Colonel's face was immobile. His hands were intertwined. Hans noticed their size and strength. They were clearly made to arouse a horse, to calm a horse, to lead a horse.

The man's eyes were fixed on the boy standing there, setting down the brown satchel as if it were full of stone.

[16] **serge**—*a thick, woolen fabric with a ribbed texture*

"Hans Haupt! Whose fault was it?" The voice was an arrow.

Hans choked out the word. "Mine."

Again that probing gaze, that arrowlike voice. "You do not blame Borina?

"Oh, no, sir. He was teaching me."

"And what about that rascal in the gallery? Was he to blame?"

"No, sir. He's no rascal; he's my nephew."

The Colonel paused. The merest wisp of a smile crossed his face. His attention seemed to wander down the aisle of stalls with the white faces and white ears listening. At last he said, "You have given the answer of a true horseman, Hans." He turned to Bereiter Wittek. "No art ever remains at the same level; rise and fall follow each other in eternal alternation.[17] Eh, Wittek?"

The Riding Master nodded, and his eyes were the mildest blue.

Hans felt a floodtide of relief. He wanted to cry, to laugh. He wanted to do pushups, handsprings.

Before he could think what to say, Colonel Podhajsky laid a hand on his shoulder. "Here is one apprentice," he said, speaking to Bereiter Wittek, "whose eye will never stray again, no matter if forty elephants wave their trunks over the gallery." With that he made a grenadier[18] turn and was gone.

Later that day a stableboy brought Hans a letter written on a square of lined school paper. In neatest penmanship the message read:

[17] **alternation**—*going back and forth from one thing to another*
[18] **grenadier** (grĕn′ə·dēr)—*a highly trained soldier known for discipline, strength, and courage*

Dear Oncle Hans,
I'm sorry I made you fall off. I did not laugh.
Your neveu, Jacques

P.S. Rosy died today also. Mon père will now buy automobil.

Hans read the letter twice. Then he re-folded it and tucked it away in his father's old satchel, in the pocket, very gently, as if it were a circlet of hairs from Rosy's tail. It was like putting away the young years of his life.

As Hans remembered Colonel Podhajsky's praise, he was even more determined to achieve his most cherished goal. Years ago, Borina famously performed ten-jump courbettes. Although Borina is now a much older horse, Hans believes that he can do it again. Will Hans and Borina be able to achieve this stunning feat? The answer lies in *White Stallion of Lipizza* by Marguerite Henry.

In the Spotlight

Jargon

1. In the first paragraph on p. 135, there are three terms of jargon related to horses. Some of these words do have other meanings that are not specific to horseback riding. What do you think they are?

2. Name terms that are jargon specific to the dressage of the stallions.

3. As Hans and Borina were "turning in a platoon," Hans fell from his horse. The general definition of platoon is *a group of people doing something together*. However, platoon has other more specific meanings in military jargon and in sports jargon. Use a dictionary to find those meanings.

I WONDER . . .

1. What did Hans dream of becoming?
2. What riding skills did Hans want to learn above all others?
3. Why was Hans permitted to take part in the performance?
4. Whose fault was it that Hans fell off his horse? Explain your answer.
5. What do you think the author meant by saying that as Hans put away the letter, "it was like putting away the young years of his life"?

THINK ON THESE THINGS

Many people have dreams and goals they want to accomplish. However, not everyone is willing to do what it takes to reach those goals. Hans wanted more than anything to become a Riding Master, and he was willing to put forth the effort required. After being accepted into the riding school, Hans realized the value of practicing and working diligently on each step without rushing through the process. Because Hans was willing to do the work and learn from his mistakes, he was able to continue his journey toward becoming a Riding Master one step at a time. Proverbs 13:4 tells us the reward of the diligent. "The soul of the sluggard desireth, and hath nothing: but the soul of the diligent shall be made fat." Hans had a great desire, but he was no sluggard; he was diligent. When we stay focused on our goals, we can defeat distraction by continuing to do the work needed to accomplish them.

If—

Rudyard Kipling

Rudyard Kipling is famous for his *Just So Stories*, a collection of short stories that includes "How the Rhinoceros Got Its Skin." Kipling wrote those imaginative selections to entertain his own children with humorous stories that are obviously untrue. The poem "If—" was written for his son John. It contains a father's wise advice about how to behave. A good author knows how to make his tone match his message. The serious tone of this poem is very different from Kipling's animal tales, but the tone is just right for this piece of good advice.

If you can keep your head when all about you
   Are losing theirs and blaming it on you;
If you can trust yourself when all men doubt you,
   But make allowance for their doubting too;
If you can wait and not be tired by waiting,
   Or being lied about, don't deal in lies,
Or being hated, don't give way to hating,
   And yet don't look too good, nor talk too wise:

If you can dream—and not make dreams your master;
   If you can think—and not make thoughts your aim;
If you can meet with Triumph and Disaster
   And treat those two impostors just the same;
If you can bear to hear the truth you've spoken
   Twisted by knaves to make a trap for fools,
Or watch the things you gave your life to, broken,
   And stoop and build 'em up with worn-out tools:

If you can talk with crowds and keep your virtue,
Or walk with Kings—nor lose the common touch,
If neither foes nor loving friends can hurt you,
If all men count with you, but none too much;
If you can fill the unforgiving minute
With sixty seconds' worth of distance run,
Yours is the Earth and everything that's in it,
And—which is more—you'll be a Man, my son!

I WONDER . . .

1. What does the poet mean when he says "keep your head when all about you are losing theirs"?
2. The Bible says we should not return evil for evil. What examples of this command do you see in this poem?
3. Why do you think the poet warns us not to "look too good, nor talk too wise"?
4. The poet has used personification in writing about triumph and disaster. How can you tell?

DEFEATING DISTRACTION WITH PURPOSE

Everyone will meet with both triumph and disaster in life. Getting carried away with triumph can lead to overconfidence, lack of dependence on God, and trouble. Being overwhelmed by disaster can cause you to give up, which is another way of not trusting God. It is good advice to face triumph and disaster equally, keeping our eyes fixed on the One Who will help us no matter the situation.

Do the Next Thing

Cheryl Reid

"I don't understand why we can't wait until the school year is over to move to Arizona," Abigail Blakely complained to her mother. "Summer will be here in two months. Does Dad really have to start his new job next week?"

"We've had this conversation several times, Abbie," her mom sighed. "I know it's not the best of circumstances, but yes, he does. All the arrangements have been made; the moving truck arrives on Monday and Dad starts his new job next Thursday. Although we might like to, we can't change any of those details."

Mrs. Blakely tried to disguise the weariness in her voice, but Abbie noticed. "I'm sorry, Mom. I know I'm complaining, but I really don't want to leave all my friends and go to a place where I don't know anyone. I'm not very good at making new friends or talking to people I don't know. I can't see myself living anywhere else. It's—it's—terrifying!"

"Believe it or not, Abbie, I'm not looking forward to that part of the move, either," Abbie's mom admitted. "When I begin to think about all the people and places I will miss, I can become discouraged and doubtful, too. At those times, we have to take control of our thoughts and our emotions and just do the next thing. Give your doubts to God; He understands."

"Give it to God—even when the next thing is five hundred miles away?"

"Yes, even then," Mrs. Blakely said, "especially then."

Abbie took some comfort in knowing that she wasn't alone in her dread of leaving the only home she had known. She continued packing up her bedroom and stacking the moving boxes in the hallway. Tomorrow, she would say goodbye to her friends, and on Tuesday, they would drive to Arizona to start a new life.

The drive to Arizona was interesting if you liked desert, sagebrush, red rocks, and mesas. The flat, straight roads seemed to go on forever. For as far as Abbie could see, there was dry, dusty landscape. Abbie already missed the springtime greenery of the Colorado mountains near her old home. *How could any part of this move be good?* she wondered. She tried to remember Mom's advice: *take control of your thoughts and emotions and just do the next thing. Give your doubts to God.*

After about eight hours in the car, Mr. Blakely pulled into the driveway of their new home. It looked much different from their Colorado home; it was covered in stucco and had a clay tile roof that would help to keep the house a little cooler during the scorching summer heat.

The moving truck arrived early the next day. Seeing their familiar furniture placed in the house helped Abbie to feel a little better. Mr. Blakely focused on getting Abbie's bed put together and her furniture arranged so she could start unpacking her things while her parents worked in the rest of the house. She tried not to think about what would happen on Friday—her first day at a new school. No matter how hard she wished Friday would never come, it did, and all too soon.

"Welcome to Palo Verde, Abigail. Let's walk down to your new classroom." Abbie quietly took in her surroundings while she followed the principal to a classroom at the end of a long hallway. She felt unsure of herself and uncomfortable about facing a room filled with people she had never seen, but here she was.

All eyes focused on Abbie as the principal ushered her into the fifth-grade classroom. The teacher, Mr. Rinehart, smiled and introduced himself and the twenty-one other students in the room as Abbie felt her face heating up with embarrassment. Mr. Rinehart showed her where she would sit and gave her a stack of textbooks. Abbie looked around the room in search of a friendly face. She met lots of stares, but no one seemed particularly glad to see a new girl. *Maybe I'll meet someone at lunch,* she thought.

Despite her hopes for lunch, things started out terribly wrong. Abbie chose spaghetti, the first thing she saw in the food line. She set the plate onto her tray and turned to find a table. At that moment, one of the boys in her class barreled into her, sending spaghetti and meat sauce onto her pink t-shirt. Abbie watched as her lunch slid down the front of her clothes and landed on the floor with a plop. For a few seconds, Abbie stood frozen in time until she heard a table of girls begin to laugh. Abbie couldn't face them. She set her tray down on the nearest table and ran to her locker to escape the situation. She opened her locker and burst into tears, sobbing in humiliation as she tried to think of a way to run out of the building without being seen. Abbie knew it was a ridiculous idea, and it was certainly not an example of taking control of her thoughts and emotions—but still.

Suddenly, Abbie heard footsteps behind her. She took a deep breath and wiped her eyes, refusing to allow anyone to see her crying over the lunch debacle. "Abigail?" a voice said.

Abbie thought of her mother's advice—take control of your thoughts and emotions, do the next thing, and give your doubts to God—and she was determined to do it. She wiped her eyes once more and turned around, ready to do the next thing. The girl who stood there was one of the girls who had laughed. "Hi. I'm Jess. I'm so sorry your shirt was ruined. I know you must be embarrassed and *hungry*. You can have my spaghetti. It's the best meal in the cafeteria. You gotta try it!"

Abbie surprised herself by smiling—until she caught a glimpse of herself in the mirror inside her locker. "Whoa! What am I going to do about this?" she moaned as she grabbed tissues from her locker and began smearing the sauce.

"How about using this cute jacket you've got hanging here? Just wipe off whatever you can, then put your jacket on over it! I speak from experience; I'm not the neatest kid in the class," Jess confessed. "And don't worry about the girls. We were laughing at the face Chase made when he ran into you. He's kind of clumsy—sometimes he trips over his own feet. The expression of terror on his face was priceless! Mr. Rinehart says Chase is like a bull in a china shop, whatever that means. He's really nice, though, and he would never want to embarrass anyone."

Jess's kindness made Abbie feel better right away. It helped to know why the girls were laughing. Wearing her jacket over the stained shirt wasn't a perfect solution, but it was still a good idea. She walked back to the lunchroom with Jess and got a new tray, but this time, she chose a simple turkey sandwich. As Abbie sat with Jess and the other girls at the table, nobody laughed at her, and they all introduced themselves. She suddenly realized how hungry she was and took a big bite of her sandwich. Looking at all the friendly faces around her, she finally understood the value of doing the next right thing.

Time to Think

1. Why was Abbie's family moving to Arizona?
2. What did Abbie learn about overcoming doubt when she opened up to her mom about her fears?
3. What was good about Abbie's reaction after meeting her new class?
4. What happened when Abbie took her mother's advice?
5. How do you think Abbie will remember this event in the future?

Why does everything have to change?

Sometimes, life surprises us with situations that feel too difficult to handle. Moving to a new school in the middle of the school year seemed way too much for Abigail. But Abigail had a wise mother who reminded her that the way to conquer doubt is to place her trust in God and allow Him to help her. Proverbs 3:6 says, "In all thy ways acknowledge Him, and He shall direct thy paths." By taking control of her emotions and giving her doubts to God, Abigail allowed God to help her conquer her doubt and trust in His plan. You can do the same. You can trust God for all the unseen future moments instead of dreading them. God is faithful and He will take care of you. We don't know the future, but we can be certain that God will be with us when we get there. Remember that no matter what may happen, whether good or bad, happy or sad, God's Word reassures us in Romans 8:28 "that all things work together for good to them that love God, to them who are the called according to His purpose." This promise is true today, tomorrow, and always.

Be Still and Know:

The Testimony of a Girl Who Gave Her Life to God

Jennifer Odom

From the time she was a child, Helen Roseveare loved helping people. Though Helen wrestled with doubts, God patiently showed His love for her again and again. When her *knowledge* of God turned to a *love* for God, she gave her life to Christ to be used for His glory. Little did Helen know of where God would take her, but she trusted God to use her, and He did in a mighty way.

Helen loved her evenings at home working math problems with her father. Mr. Roseveare was a mathematician who taught at various schools. "Father, why is it important to learn my lessons and work so hard at them?" Helen asked.

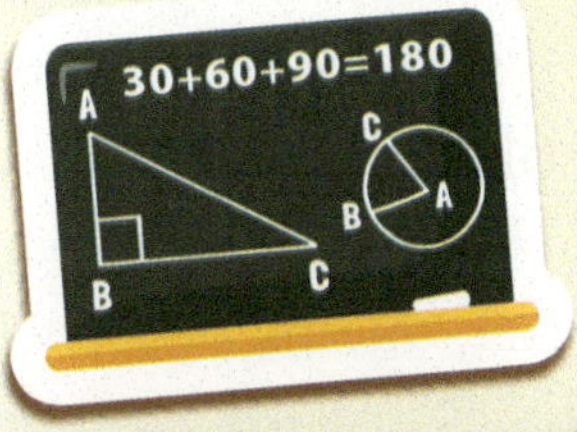

"Because whatever task God gives you to do, it is always right to do your very best for Him," answered her father. Although Helen didn't fully understand her father's reason, she determined to work hard.

Helen was born in 1925 in Hertfordshire, England. She was the second of five children. In 1937, when Helen was twelve years old, she was sent to a boarding school in North Wales. Because Helen excelled in most everything she did, the other girls did not like her very much. Helen did not let it stop her, however, and she continued working very hard.

Through her hard work, Helen won the top academic award at school three years in a row.

"We are so proud of you," said her father. "You give your family a good name!" her mother said with a beaming smile. While pleasing those we love is a worthy goal, eventually, Helen would come to realize that Jesus is the One to please first and foremost.

At the end of World War II, Helen enrolled in Cambridge University to study medicine. The first few weeks of university were difficult for her. She was close to her family and missed them terribly. She felt alone and began doubting God's existence. Homesickness and loneliness were settling in on her, one night especially. Helen noticed a small card on the mirror in her room. She picked it up to read, "If you have no other plans or anyone else to be with tonight, come to room no. 8 at 8:00 p.m. for coffee. Dorothy." Helen wondered who Dorothy was, but she had no plans and no one else to be with. So, she mustered up the courage to go to room no. 8 to meet Dorothy.

Helen knocked on the door of room no. 8 timidly. She almost walked away, but before she could, a cheery voice called out, "Come in!" There was a friendly looking girl inside making last-minute preparations for her guests. "Hello there. I'm Dorothy, and I'm so glad you came!" Helen immediately felt at ease, and a friendship began that would change Helen's life forever.

Helen didn't realize that Dorothy and her friends loved Jesus and gathered weekly to talk about Him and learn more about His Word. Helen watched the girls' lives and the way they spoke of God as if they knew Him personally. Helen was curious, but she still was not quite sure what she thought of the whole matter. Dorothy and her friends began praying for Helen.

"I won't be able to go home for Christmas this year because my younger sister has the mumps," Helen told Dorothy, sadly.

"You should go with us to a Bible conference. You will love it!" exclaimed Dorothy. Helen went with the girls, and it was there she came to understand clearly the Gospel for the first time.

After having only been at the conference for one day, Helen was under great conviction. She left the dinner table in tears, ran upstairs to her room, and threw herself across the bed. "Lord," Helen cried, "if You are real, please make Yourself known to me now!" Helen looked up in front of her and saw a Bible verse on the wall. The ceiling had leaked, and the last word had been washed away. It simply read, "Be still and know that I am. . . ."

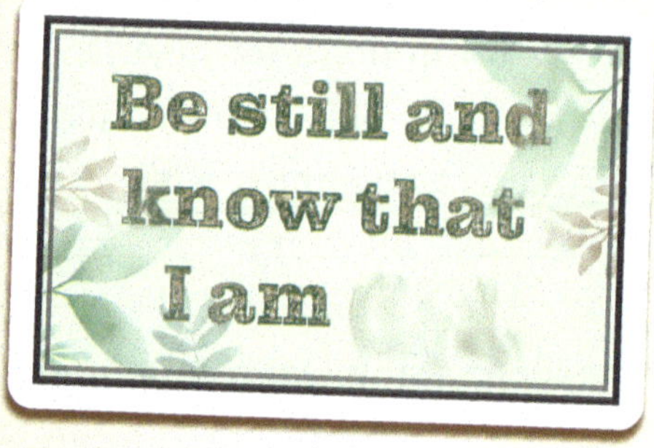

Helen was overwhelmed that God, Whom she had learned so much about, had taken the time to speak to her wondering heart. Helen realized that God the Creator loved her, cared for her, and had a purpose for her, and not only for her, but also for everyone else. When she understood that God had sent His Son to die for her sins, it completely changed her life. Now, Helen wanted to give her life to share the Good News with others.

"There is such a difference in Helen," her friends said. "We can see it on her face!" From then on, Helen wouldn't live to please people; it was her Savior that she would live to please!

On February 13, 1953, after having graduated from Cambridge University, Helen left London to go to the Belgian Congo in Africa (the modern-day Democratic Republic of the Congo), as a medical missionary. A crowd of her family and friends were at the train station to see her off. As the train made its way down the track, Helen watched them fade off in the distance. The young missionary girl was filled with both nervousness and excitement at what lay before her.

When Helen arrived at the end of her journey, both the American missionaries and the African people were there to greet her. Right away, Helen felt loved, and, even more importantly, she felt needed. There was much work to do, and Helen got busy right away.

With Helen overseeing much of the project, a new hospital was soon built where Helen could begin offering

medical services to the people living nearby. Many of these people were also able to hear about the Great Physician, Who would give them the greatest healing of all. Soon, Helen earned the endearing nickname Mama Luka—named after Luke, the physician in the New Testament, who wrote one of the Gospels.

Helen lay in bed one night when suddenly she heard someone at her door. "Mama Luka, come quickly! We need your help!" Helen rushed to the hospital where she found a young mother expecting a child. Unfortunately, the young mother died after her premature baby was born. She left behind the tiny baby and a two-year-old daughter.

"Go get the hot-water bottle and fill it up with boiling water," Helen instructed her assistant. "We must keep this baby warm, or she will die."

In a few minutes' time, the young assistant came back in tears. "I'm so sorry, Mama Luka, but when I boiled the water and poured it in the hot-water bottle, the bottle burst. It was our last one!" Helen assured the nurse that God would help them. Helen instructed her to wrap the baby in a warm blanket and put it as close to the fire as she safely could. The nurses all took turns throughout the night staying awake to make sure the baby stayed warm.

The next morning, Helen went to the nearby orphanage for prayer time with the orphan children, as she did every day. She gave them a few things for which to pray. "Children, we must pray that God will help the nurses to stay awake all night long to keep the baby warm. If she does not stay warm enough, she will die." Helen told them of the hot-water bottle, and the little two-year-old girl who was crying because she missed her mommy.

As the children took turns praying for different things, Ruth, a ten-year-old orphan girl, prayed, "God, please send a hot-water bottle today so the baby can stay warm. If it comes tomorrow, it will be no good; please send it today. If it comes tomorrow, the baby will die. And please God, while you are at it, send a dolly for the big sister so she will know that Jesus loves her too."

Helen swallowed hard—that was a prayer she did not believe could be answered. In the four years she had been in this part of the Congo, she had never received a crate from home. Later that afternoon, a truck drove up to their village and dropped off a large crate for Helen from back home in England!

Helen felt a lump in her throat and knew she could not open the parcel by herself. She called the orphan children, and they all gathered around. As they began to unpack the crate, on top were bandages, soap, and other supplies. Helen put her hand back into the crate and pulled out a new hot-water bottle. Although Helen lived near the equator where it is warm, someone back home in England had decided to send her a hot-water bottle!

Ruth, the little girl who had prayed, rushed forward. "Mama Luka, if God sent the hot-water bottle, He must have sent the dolly too!" Sure enough, at the bottom of the crate was a dolly that someone had included.

As Helen realized that the crate would have been packed and sent five months earlier, her faith and gratitude toward God grew even deeper. God had already provided the answer to a ten-year-old girl's prayer five months earlier and delivered it the very day she prayed! Helen and all the orphans learned a faith-building lesson that day. God knows our need before we ask and will always provide at just the right time.

Helen Roseveare served in the Belgian Congo for twenty years. In those years she saw many victories and endured some very dark days. However, through it all, she kept her faith in God and depended on the very One she told others about. Helen died at the age of 91 on December 7, 2016. She left behind a beautiful legacy of faith and service to her Lord and the African people, who lovingly called her Mama Luka.

IN THE SPOTLIGHT

Text Structure

1. The text structure the author used to communicate the time order of Helen's life is ____.
   a. chronological
   b. compare/contrast
   c. descriptive
2. Why are biographical stories often written in this text structure?

I WONDER . . .

1. How did Helen's motivation and desire to please people change throughout her life?
2. What doubts did Helen have about God, and how were her doubts relieved?
3. Why would Helen use her talent and knowledge to spread the Gospel?

God still speaks to us just as He spoke to Helen through His Word. "Be still, and know that I am God" comes from Psalm 46:10. If you're wondering how you can be a friend of God, be still. Ask Him to speak to you through His Word when it is taught or read. He will. He wants to be your friend.

To focus on Creative Writing, see pages 206–207.

Little Seeds

Located right below the country of Mexico, Guatemala is one of the largest countries of Central America. Guatemala City is the most populated area in the country. Its hundreds of neighborhoods bustle[1] with activity! Every morning, the neighborhood bakery crowds with people buying bread to eat with breakfast and lunch. The tortilla vendor walks around the neighborhood selling fresh, hot corn tortillas from a cloth-wrapped basket carried on her head. The knife sharpener blows a special tune on his panpipes to alert the neighborhood that he is ready to sharpen their kitchen knives. Many merchants roam Guatemalan neighborhoods, but the favorite one by far is the ice-cream man pushing a striped umbrella-shaded cart full of frozen treats. When boys and girls hear his bell ringing, they run to buy fudge bars or ice-cream sandwiches on a hot day. One such child, a dark-eyed, ten-year-old girl named Ximena,[2] lived in a neighborhood just like this one.

Ximena lived on the upper floor of an apartment building in Guatemala City with her parents and her younger brothers Juan José[3] and José Jorge.[4] From their apartment's glittering windows, they had a striking view. In the distance, blue ridges of mountain ranges rose to the sky. Sometimes clouds masked the tops of three cone-shaped volcanoes that could be seen among the mountains. Nearer, lush green trees blanketed the hillsides, with skyscrapers, stores, and homes rising above the landscape. Ximena's apartment building was called

[1] **bustle**—*move about with energetic activity*
[2] **Ximena** (hee-**men**-uh)
[3] **Juan** (hwahn) **José** (ho-**seh**)
[4] **Jorge** (**hor**-heh)

El Parque[5] because across the street was a beautiful tree-filled park with walking paths, a playground, and a large pavilion.

The three children loved to go to the park. Juan José, who was now eight, raced his red bicycle with his sister, and, because little José Jorge in his blue overalls could not keep up with them on his tricycle, he blew a whistle, held up his hand, and squealed, "Stop!" pretending to be the traffic control officer. Sometimes the children enjoyed picnics spread out on a mint-green and pink cloth on the grass. Better than the grassy field for playing and picnics, though, was a large orange brick pavilion with open sides and a roof crowned with ivy and small white flowers. Because Ximena's family loved to share the Gospel with their friends and neighbors, Ximena's mother held a

[5] **El Parque** (el **par**-keh)—*Spanish for "the park"*

weekly Bible club at the pavilion for boys and girls after school on Mondays. Eventually the Bible club was called *Semillitas*[6] because the seeds of the Gospel were being spread to the children in the neighborhood.

Bible club in the park

While Ximena's father was still at work in his office, her mother picked up Ximena, Juan José, and José Jorge from school and drove to the pavilion where they prepared for Bible club. Little José Jorge carried a box of snacks from the van, while Juan José set up chairs. Ximena and her mother set up tables and an easel with the flannel board for the Bible story. Soon other mothers arrived at the park with children wearing school uniforms. Some mothers brought snacks; others brought lemonade or water to drink. All ages from kindergarten through the sixth grade were welcome. As the children sang songs or played games, other neighborhood boys and girls were attracted to the pavilion. For two hours each Monday, twenty or more boys and girls stayed to join the fun and hear the Bible story. The children loved playing with friends, eating snacks, singing songs, and learning about God.

---

[6] **Semillitas** (se-mee-**yee**-tahs)—*Spanish for "little seeds"*

In His Word, the Lord promises that He will provide for every need, and God always provided for the needs of the Bible club. Because Ximena's mother seldom knew ahead of time how many children might come, she sometimes wondered if she had enough snacks for all the children. Once, she accidentally asked four mothers instead of two to bring snacks and found that she had double of everything. That day, when twice as many children came to the Bible club, there were enough snacks and drinks for everyone! God took care of a need that Ximena's mother did not even know she was going to have. Just as He did when Jesus fed 5,000 people from a young boy's lunch, God provided so that the children could learn of Him.

On another occasion, Ximena's mother realized that she had run out of time to buy glue for the craft project. After picking up Ximena, Juan José, and José Jorge from school, she asked them, "Please pray that God will provide a solution for the lack of glue." She brushed back her wavy blonde hair from her worried eyes, and the children prayed aloud as their mother drove. At the park, they helped carry the supplies to the pavilion as usual. A few minutes later, one of the Bible club helpers arrived with a large white shopping bag. "While I was at the store today," Jackie explained, placing the bag on the table, "I felt the need to bring glue and paper to Semillitas." Ximena's mother's worried face transformed into a grateful smile as she hugged her friend. She called her children over to the craft table. "Come see what Jackie brought! See how God answered our prayers!" she exclaimed. Although Jackie usually helped provide the snacks, God had used her to meet the

Ximena (left) with Bible club friends

special need for the craft project. Now they would be able to make a craft of Peter walking on the water. The children's faith in God's provision mirrored Peter's faith and Jesus' care of Peter's needs. Over and over, Ximena and her family saw God supply needs for the Bible club. As the leaders and helpers faithfully shared Gospel seeds of truth from the Bible with the neighborhood children, many boys and girls accepted God's forgiveness of sin and trusted in Jesus as their Savior.

Each time doubt arose, Ximena's family would remember God's faithfulness in providing the children, the help, the snacks, and the glue, and they would trust Him to provide—just as He always had.

Ximena's parents were not called to be missionaries to another country. God did not impress on her father to be a pastor or to start a Christian school. God's plan for Ximena's family was to tell the Good News of salvation to their friends and neighbors in Guatemala City.

The family understood that the Gospel is meant to be shared with others and lived out every day. Everyone needs to hear about God's love, forgiveness, and faithfulness, starting with the people right in their own neighborhood.

Time to Think

1. Where does this story take place?
2. How did Ximena's family share the Gospel with the people in her neighborhood?
3. How did God supply the needs for Semillitas?
4. Is "Little Seeds" a good name for the club? Why or Why not?

Think on These Things

Ximena's family did not have a special building to use for the Semillitas Bible Club; they had a neighborhood park. From there they planted the "seeds" of the Gospel. At the same time, Ximena and her family learned that they could trust God to take care of their needs—big or small.

God gives each of us unique opportunities to share His love with others. What seeds can you plant? What light can you shine? What can you use to help point friends and neighbors to Christ?

"Ye are the light of the world. A city that is set on an hill cannot be hid. Neither do men light a candle, and put it under a bushel, but on a candlestick; and it giveth light unto all that are in the house. Let your light so shine before men, that they may see your good works, and glorify your Father which is in Heaven." —Matthew 5:14–16

Savior, WHILE MY HEART IS TENDER

John Burton, Jr.

Savior, while my heart is tender,
I would yield that heart to Thee;
All my pow'rs to Thee surrender,[1]
Thine and only Thine to be.
Take me now, Lord Jesus, take me,
Let my youthful heart be Thine,
Thy devoted[2] servant make me,
Fill my soul with love divine.

Send me, Lord, where Thou wilt send me,
Only do Thou guide my way,
May Thy grace thro' life attend me,
Cheerfully will I obey.
Let me do Thy will, or bear it,
I would know no will but Thine,
Shouldst Thou take my life, or spare it,
I that life to Thee resign.[3]

May this solemn consecration[4]
Never once forgotten be;
Let it know no revocation,[5]
Registered, confirmed by Thee.
Thine I am, O Lord, forever
To Thy service set apart;
Suffer me to leave Thee never,
Seal Thine image on my heart.

---

[1] **surrender**—*hand over; yield*
[2] **devoted**—*dedicated*
[3] **resign**—*submit*
[4] **consecration**—*to be set apart for service*
[5] **revocation**—*the act of canceling or taking back*

Time to Think

1. Why do you think it is important to have and to keep a tender heart?
2. How does the first stanza foreshadow a time when the heart may no longer be tender toward the Lord?
3. How does the third stanza encourage the young person to remain tender to the Lord?

Guatemalan Cocadas*

Yields two dozen

Cocadas are a South American dessert made with coconut. In the past, these desserts were extremely popular near the coasts because coconuts could easily be found there. Nowadays, however, these desserts are popular throughout Guatemala. Follow the simple recipe below to get your own taste of Guatemalan cuisine!

Ingredients and Materials:

- 2 tablespoons of water
- 1 cup flour
- 2 eggs
- 5 cups shredded coconut
- 1 cup sweetened condensed milk
- ½ teaspoon vanilla extract
- parchment paper
- spoon or cookie scoop

Instructions:

First, preheat oven to 350°F. Then, cover a baking sheet with parchment paper to prevent the cocadas from sticking to the baking sheet.

Next, add the water, flour, and eggs to a large bowl. Stir until the batter is smooth and free from clumps.

* **cocadas** (koh-**kah**-dahs)—*coconut confections or sweet treats*

Then, add the shredded coconut, sweetened condensed milk, and vanilla extract to the batter. Stir until all the ingredients are mixed together evenly.

Next, use a spoon or cookie scoop to form a one-inch ball for each cookie.

Place the balls of batter onto the parchment-covered sheet. Bake for 20 minutes or until the cocadas have turned golden brown.

Once the cocadas are finished baking, allow them to fully cool before serving.

Time to Think

1. What is the purpose of this recipe?
   a. to retell a sequence of events
   b. to reveal a problem and solution
   c. to show a step-by-step process
2. Which text structure was used to write the recipe instructions?
3. Why might it be important to mix the ingredients in order?
4. What are cocadas, and how many can you make with this recipe?

The Battle Is the Lord's

based on 2 Chronicles 20:1–22

About sixty years after Israel was divided into two kingdoms, Israel and Judah, Jehoshaphat became the king of Judah. The Bible tells us that like his ancestor King David, Jehoshaphat did "that which was right in the sight of the LORD." However, even those who try to do right face difficult challenges. In this passage, Jehoshaphat has received bad news: enemy forces are gathering and preparing to attack. The king knows he and his army are not adequate to face this foe. Where will he turn for help?

King Jehoshaphat gazed at Jerusalem's surrounding hills as he thought of the unwelcome news he had just received. *Armies of enemy soldiers have been spotted nearby! We must prepare for battle!* A great multitude was advancing toward Jerusalem in the land of Judah. The Moabites and Ammonites, cruel enemies of Judah, had marched from the East along with an army from Mount Seir and joined forces to fight against God's people.

King Jehoshaphat was not a perfect man, but he trusted in God and lived by His commandments. He instructed his people in the ways of the Lord. The countries surrounding Judah knew of King Jehoshaphat's trust in and loyalty to God. Even though Jehoshaphat had a large army, this surprising news of an enemy attack caused him to be fearful. But then he remembered the great power of his God. He cried out to God for help and called on the people of Judah to do the

same. The king declared that the people should fast and pray, asking God to protect them and deliver them from their enemies.

Following their king's example, the people of Judah gathered together at the Temple where they worshiped God. They came from cities all over the land of Judah to pray for God's help and protection. Fathers, mothers, and children all stood together before their king. While the people listened, King Jehoshaphat prayed. "God, You rule over all the kingdoms of the earth! You have all power and might! No one is able to stand against

You! You are God, Who gave us this land. You have promised to help us in our need. Now our enemies have come to fight. Help us, God, for we do not know what to do. We look only to You!"

Everyone was quiet after the king's prayer. The people waited. King Jehoshaphat waited. They knew that their faithful God would hear and answer their prayer. Then a man began to speak. Jahaziel was a Temple musician who led the people of Judah in songs of worship to God. God gave Jahaziel His message for the people. "Listen to what the Lord says to you! Do not be afraid of the enemy soldiers. The battle is not yours; the battle is the Lord's! Go and meet the enemy tomorrow; you will find them by the brook near the wilderness of Jeruel. You will not fight this battle; you will stand still and see the salvation of the Lord! He is with you!"

King Jehoshaphat knew that this message truly came from God. When he bowed down to worship, all the people bowed with him to thank and praise God for His promise of victory. Then the singers stood up to praise God with loud, strong voices. God had promised them victory without a battle! How could this be? They did not know, but they had faith to believe what God said.

Early the next morning, the army of Judah rose and followed God's instructions. As the men walked to face the enemy, King Jehoshaphat reminded them to have faith in God's promises. Then the king did something very unusual for an army heading to face its enemies. He decided that singers should lead the army! "Sing songs about God's beauty and holiness! Praise Him because His mercy endures forever!" the king told them. As the

singers marched ahead of the soldiers, the army may have joined in the songs of praise and worship to God.

Perhaps as the soldiers marched, they remembered what they had heard about the battle of Jericho many years earlier. God had given victory in an unusual way there. After marching around the walled city seven times in silence, God told the Israelites to shout, and then He caused the walls of the city to fall. The army of Judah understood that God sometimes worked in ways that men would not.

As the voices of the singers filled the air with praise to God, the Lord kept His promise. Just as God had said, the army of Judah did not have to fight at all. That day, there was great rejoicing in the land of Judah! Their faithful God delivered His people from their enemies and protected them from any harm.

2 Chronicles 20:1–22

1 It came to pass after this also, that the children of
Moab, and the children of Ammon, and with them other
beside the Ammonites, came against Jehoshaphat to
battle. 2 Then there came some that told Jehoshaphat,
saying, There cometh a great multitude against thee from
beyond the sea on this side Syria; and, behold, they be
in Hazazon-tamar, which is En-gedi. 3 And Jehoshaphat
feared, and set himself to seek the LORD, and proclaimed
a fast throughout all Judah. 4 And Judah gathered them-
selves together, to ask help of the LORD: even out of all the
cities of Judah they came to seek the LORD.

5 And Jehoshaphat stood in the congregation of Judah
and Jerusalem, in the house of the LORD, before the new
court, 6 and said, O LORD God of our fathers, art not Thou
God in heaven? and rulest not Thou over all the kingdoms
of the heathen? and in Thine hand is there not power and
might, so that none is able to withstand Thee? 7 Art not
Thou our God, Who didst drive out the inhabitants of this
land before Thy people Israel, and gavest it to the seed of
Abraham Thy friend for ever? 8 And they dwelt therein,
and have built Thee a sanctuary therein for Thy name,
saying, 9 If, when evil cometh upon us, as the sword,
judgment, or pestilence, or famine, we stand before
this house, and in Thy presence, (for Thy name is in this
house,) and cry unto Thee in our affliction, then Thou
wilt hear and help. 10 And now, behold, the children of
Ammon and Moab and mount Seir, whom Thou wouldest

not let Israel invade, when they came out of the land of Egypt, but they
turned from them, and destroyed them not; 11 behold, I say, how they
reward us, to come to cast us out of Thy possession, which Thou hast
given us to inherit. 12 O our God, wilt Thou not judge them? for we have
no might against this great company that cometh against us; neither
know we what to do: but our eyes are upon Thee. 13 And all Judah stood
before the LORD, with their little ones, their wives, and their children.

14 Then upon Jahaziel the son of Zechariah, the son of Benaiah, the
son of Jeiel, the son of Mattaniah, a Levite of the sons of Asaph, came
the Spirit of the LORD in the midst of the congregation; 15 and he said,
Hearken ye, all Judah, and ye inhabitants of Jerusalem, and Thou king
Jehoshaphat, Thus saith the LORD unto you, Be not afraid nor dismayed
by reason of this great multitude; for the battle is not yours, but God's.
16 Tomorrow go ye down against them: behold, they come up by the cliff
of Ziz; and ye shall find them at the end of the brook, before the wilder-
ness of Jeruel. 17 Ye shall not need to fight in this battle: set yourselves,
stand ye still, and see the salvation of the LORD with you, O Judah and
Jerusalem: fear not, nor be dismayed; tomorrow go out against them:
for the LORD will be with you. 18 And Jehoshaphat bowed his head with
his face to the ground: and all Judah and the inhabitants of Jerusalem
fell before the LORD, worshiping the LORD. 19 And the Levites, of the
children of the Kohathites, and of the children of the Korhites, stood up
to praise the LORD God of Israel with a loud voice on high.

20 And they rose early in the morning, and went forth into the wilder-
ness of Tekoa: and as they went forth, Jehoshaphat stood and said,
Hear me, O Judah, and ye inhabitants of Jerusalem; Believe in the LORD
your God, so shall ye be established; believe His prophets, so shall ye
prosper. 21 And when he had consulted with the people, he appointed
singers unto the LORD, and that should praise the beauty of holiness,
as they went out before the army, and to say, Praise the LORD; for His
mercy endureth for ever.

22 And when they began to sing and to praise, the LORD set ambushments against the children of Ammon, Moab, and mount Seir, which were come against Judah; and they were smitten.

I WONDER . . .

1. When we compare the Scripture passage from 2 Chronicles 20 to "The Battle Is the Lord's," which of the following statements are true?
   a. They are both narratives.
   b. 2 Chronicles 20 is Scripture; God is the author.
   c. "The Battle Is the Lord's" is based on 2 Chronicles 20; it is man's retelling of God's Word.
   d. Some elements of the retelling in "The Battle Is the Lord's" are imagined by the author.
2. In what country did Jehoshaphat rule as king?
3. What unwelcome news did King Jehoshaphat receive?
4. What did King Jehoshaphat remember that helped him not to be afraid?
5. In what unusual way did the soldiers march toward the battle?
6. What had God promised His people?

THINK ON THESE THINGS

Everyone faces difficult situations at times. In those times, our reactions reveal who or what we trust. Fear is often our first human reaction. If we're not careful, fear can turn to doubt. Like King Jehoshaphat, we must remind ourselves of God's power. Placing trust in our all-powerful God relieves fear and gives us hope in His promises.

After the king's prayer, he and his people waited quietly. Why is it important to patiently wait for God's answer to our prayers?

HE IS MY REFUGE

Author Unknown

The Lord is my Refuge
My Haven[1] from storm,
My Strength in all weakness,
My Peace in alarm,
My Joy in all sorrow,
My Hope in despair,
My Courage in conquest,
My Helper in prayer.

The Lord is my Fortress,
To Him I can go
When all others fail me,
And waters o'erflow.
The Lord is my Buckler[2]
He's strong to defend,
My Rock of salvation,
My Hope to the end.

So what though the mountains
Be moved to the sea,
Or the heavens above
Should cease there to be;
Or friends may forsake me,
And Satan my foe,
Be strong to uproot me;
He's with me I know!

[1] **haven**—*shelter*
[2] **buckler**—*a shield*

I WONDER . . .

1. What is another word for refuge?
2. How is the Lord a refuge for you?

 To focus on Figurative Language, see page 208.

The Great Storm

from *Abbie Burgess: Lighthouse Heroine*
by Dorothy Holder Jones and Ruth Sexton Sargent

Abigail Burgess lived with her parents and younger sisters on the Rock, a tiny island off the coast of Maine. Mr. Burgess was the lighthouse keeper, and Abbie helped him tend the lights in the two towers connected to their stone house. In this true story, we learn how Abbie cared not only for the lights but also for her sisters and ailing[1] mother when Mr. Burgess had to leave for supplies during the winter of 1856.

The girls stamped about in their snowshoes for over an hour, pelting one another with snowballs and playing with the hens. While they were eating dinner, the kitchen became so dark that Abbie got up to light the lamp. As she did so, a gust of wind whined down the

[1] **ailing**—*having an illness; sickly*

chimney, followed by a blast that set the shutters slamming furiously against the house.

She ran to the window. The clear sky had deepened to an ominous dark gray. Gulls screamed wildly. From the way the flag on the pole was blowing, she knew the wind had veered to the northeast.

Esther and Mahala[2] began to cry, and Mrs. Burgess called out from the parlor, "Abigail, your father's caught in this storm!"

"Now, Mother, he's halfway to the mainland by now. And it may be just a gale[3] that'll blow right out to sea."

Esther and Mahala rushed in to them. "What'll we do, Abbie?" Esther asked worriedly.

"We'll do exactly what Father would if he were here. We'll batten things down." She directed Lydia and Esther to latch all the shutters, and Mahala was sent to bring in the flag.

Abbie closed up the sheds and moved the hen coop to a more protected spot. After all was done, her sisters sat around the fire, complaining about being alone on the Rock without their father.

"Now Father can't bring back the supplies until the storm's over," Lydia whined. "And that might be several days!"

"We won't dwell on that," Abbie told her. "We'll take each day as it comes. I'd best light the lamps early today. It's so dark."

With each hour, the wind grew more frenzied, until it was battering the Rock unmercifully. Huge breakers[4] flung themselves at the ledges.

---

[2] **Mahala** (mə·hā′lə)

[3] **gale**—*a very strong wind*

[4] **breakers**—*crashing waves that break into foam*

Abbie lost count of the hours she spent minding the lamps. In between her vigil,[5] she kept her loved ones warm and fed, and calmed their fears. At night, Mahala slept with Mrs. Burgess, and Lydia and Esther spread pallets by the fireside. Abbie, exhausted from her labors, was glad to have the comfort of the couch.

For a week, there was no relief from the hurricane winds. It was as though the elements[6] had gone mad and were venting all their fury upon the Rock. On the eighth morning, Abbie was awakened by a loud boom. She sat up, every nerve taut.[7] A breaker had slammed against the house!

She hurried up to the tower and was relieved to find the lamps still glowing. The sky was so dark, she let the lamps burn on, though the oil was scarce. In the light the towers cast, she could see gray billows heaving offshore. Each one rose higher than the one before it, and splashed farther upon the Rock.

When Abbie returned to the kitchen, she found Lydia struggling to help Esther make a batch of griddle cakes. Mahala was using towels to mop up water from a leak under the kitchen door. They all turned to Abbie with frightened faces.

"It's worse," Lydia said, her lips quivering.

Mahala shouted, "Are we going to be washed away?"

"Not likely." Abbie tried to smile. "After we eat, things won't seem so gloomy."

The morning passed swiftly and without incident, but just as they began to eat dinner, a breaker crashed on the roof with the boom of a cannon. They clung to each

---

5 **vigil**—*keeping watch during normal sleeping hours*
6 **elements**—*weather forces; especially severe weather*
7 **taut**—*tight*

other in terror, as if waiting for the end. Time passed, and there was only a terrible, deafening roar.

When the furor[8] quieted some, Abbie sprang to her feet. "Mother, the coop is bound to be flooded. I must get my hens before they drown—"

Her mother grabbed her dress. "Abigail, you daren't go outside! You'll be swept right out to sea!"

"But I can't bear to part with my hens. If I go before another breaker comes—there's a chance."

She grabbed a basket, and when the sea fell back a little, she ran down the steps. The water came up to her knees, but she pushed on until she came to the coop. She opened the door, and the hens tumbled out. She scooped two into the basket, and the others flapped about frantically. Two white feathery forms were sinking into the water, but she pulled them out and dropped them into the basket.

[8]**furor**—*frenzy; rage*

Mahala opened the back door, and Abbie dashed inside. A gigantic billow, about thirty feet in height, was lunging toward the Rock.

"Close the door!" Abbie yelled.

Mahala screamed and shut the door. Abbie flung the basket down, the hens scattering, and hurried to the chest of drawers near the door.

"Help me bar the door!" she cried, pushing against the weight of the heavy chest. Her sisters came and pitted their strength with hers, and the chest slid in front of the door just as the breaker struck. The house trembled from the impact. They leaned limply against the chest, certain this was the final blow.

After a moment, when it appeared the house had survived, Mrs. Burgess burst into sobs. The younger girls ran to her, while Lydia took pity on the squawking hens and gathered them into her lap.

Abbie went to check to see what damage had been done. Entering the tower, she stepped into a pool of water. She held her breath and quickly opened the door leading to the wooden chamber beside the tower, where her mother had slept before they moved her into the parlor. She gasped. The space where the room had been was an abyss of swirling water. Only the stone foundation stood. She shut the door and leaned against it as horror filled her mind. Her mother might have been in that room!

She took stock of the situation. The ocean had already washed away the wooden section of the house, and if the storm got any worse, the house itself might not stand. The towers, she decided, were their only chance.

As they were finishing their evening meal, she said, "Mother, we'd best move into the tower until the storm's over. The lamp room would be right comfortable."

"The tower!" Lydia interrupted. "It smells horrid in there!"

"We'd freeze," Esther put in.

Mrs. Burgess shook her head. "Abigail, I won't let anyone sleep up there."

"The lamps give a lot of heat," Abbie pointed out.

"But there's no sense going up there, Abigail."

Abbie sighed. "Then I'm obliged to tell you," she said, struggling to keep her voice steady. "The—the wooden chamber was washed away this morning. The timbers are probably strewn about Penobscot Bay[9] right now. I figure the towers are stronger than the house. We'll be safer there."

Lydia continued to protest, and Abbie's mother insisted she couldn't endure the climb up the tower stairs. Abbie argued with them until she was hoarse.

She put soapstones[10] on top of the stove to heat, to help keep their feet warm. She collected the bedding and a basket of food, and when all was ready, she led the two younger girls up to the tower off the kitchen. When she had them settled comfortably in the lamp room, she went back down and asked her mother once more.

"No, Abigail," she replied, "I'll stay here and keep the fire going. Lydia can stay with me."

Abbie went back to the tower, knowing that if things worsened, they'd come up to the lamp room. When she entered, with a lamp in one hand and the family Bible

---

[9] **Penobscot Bay** (pə·nŏb′skət)

[10] **soapstones**—*a soft stone composed mostly of talc that has a soapy feel*

in the other, Mahala asked, "What did you bring the Bible for?"

"So I can read it," she said. "Father reads the Bible every night, doesn't he?"

The lamp room, though ten feet in diameter, was small compared to the kitchen, so Abbie was able to speak in a more normal tone. She turned to the passages in the seventh chapter of Matthew where Jesus spoke about the house built upon a rock. She read it with conviction, then explained to her sisters that the rock to which the Master referred was the rock of faith.

"We must have faith that the house will survive and that Father will return safely."

Sometime after they were finally asleep, Abbie donned the oilskins and boots she'd brought up to the tower. After another breaker passed overhead, she quickly went out on the catwalk to scrape the windows before the next breaker struck.

The wind screamed and buffeted her against the tower, and needles of ice pricked her cheeks. The ocean lapped viciously below the tower, as though it were a monster eager to swallow the house and towers. Knowing that her next step might be into eternity, she prayed.

With the below-zero temperatures, the ocean spray froze instantly on the glass panes, yet there was only a thin layer of ice on each window. The heat from the lamps inside, she decided, kept the windows slightly warm. The warning grumble of another breaker sent her back inside.

On the next try, she finished scraping all the windows. She rested a spell, then began the journey to the other tower. It seemed peculiar not to hear her own footsteps, for in good weather, her feet fairly boomed in the granite tower. But tonight, it was as though she walked on velvet.

She went on through the house, passing her mother, who was sleeping on the couch, and Lydia stretched on a pallet nearby. She climbed up to the second tower. Out on the second catwalk, she clung to the railing, not daring to look down at the swirling water below. She began to sing a hymn, and its words gave her the courage to complete her task.

Back in the first tower, she snuggled close to her sleeping sisters and closed her eyes. She wondered drowsily if Mr. Pratt had put her father up for the night.

She dozed only, waking at intervals to check the lamps; then she'd drop off again. All of a sudden, she felt someone shaking her. She sat up and saw Lydia, holding the lamp from the kitchen table. Her mouth was moving, but no sound came out.

This must be what it's like to be deaf, Abbie thought giddily[11] as she realized the storm had worsened. Lydia screamed into her ear. "The kitchen's flooding, Abbie! You must come!"

Abbie got to her feet, stiff and cold, and followed Lydia into the kitchen. Putting her mother's arm across her shoulders, Abbie supported her weight as they mounted the stairs. No heavy work she'd done for her father compared to the exertion of that climb. With her last bit of energy, she arranged the bedding.

"Mercy," her mother moaned. "I wish your father was here. I'm too sick to help you, and you don't have the strength—"

---

[11] **giddily**—*dizzily*

Abbie patted her shoulder. "God will give me the strength to do my duty, Mother. You sleep now."

"It's a good thing you've got such faith, Abigail. We'll all be needing it before this is over."

Abbie slept for a little while, then awoke to attend to the lamps. Wrapped in the oilskins, she went down to the kitchen. The parlor was flooded now, but she walked through it. The lamps in the second tower flickered as she entered, but blazed right up again.

The wind had an eerie, high-pitched whine as Abbie stepped out on the catwalk, and the water still churned below. She chipped at the icy windows until her hands began to ache despite her thick gloves.

At the first streak of dawn, she snuffed out the lamps, eager to save the precious oil. The ocean's fury was still blasting the Rock, but it was easier to bear in daylight, Abbie discovered.

She managed to build a fire in the stove and put on a pot of cornmeal mush. In between the breakers, she swept salt water out of the kitchen door. Then she built a fire in the fireplace. When the room was fairly warm, she brought the others down.

Once their stomachs were filled, everyone cheered up a little—even dozed a while. But the day was a mixture of gratitude and discomfort. The house had withstood the onslaught, but its furnishings were soaked. Their food supply was dangerously low, and there was no relief in sight.

Abbie flew the flag at half-mast, with the hope that some ship, plowing through the rough waters, might think it a signal of distress and send some supplies to them. But they saw no ship.

In the days that followed, Mrs. Burgess kept to her bed, so Abbie was in full charge of the household and the lamps. She gave Lydia the task of attending to their mother's needs, and Esther and Mahala were to keep the kitchen clean and warm.

Abbie encouraged them all to carry on with their handiwork, and she tutored them and read the Bible to them every night. The busier she kept them, the less they complained about their hunger, for she now had to cut down on everyone's rations[12] in order to stretch the food.

Throughout the days, she thought of her father. He'll come today, for sure, she'd tell herself each morning. He *must* come today. I'm so tired, and there's so little to eat.

The storm continued to rage for two weeks. The ocean never broke over the Rock again, but angry breakers pounded steadily, spraying the windows of the house. Abbie lost sleep and rest, but she kept on. If God would give her the strength, she would keep the lamps burning.

In mid-February, the ocean receded. Abbie opened the shutters, and for the first time in weeks, daylight flooded in.

A few evenings later, when she was up in the tower checking the lamps, Abbie noticed a tiny light offshore. She wasted no time getting down to the landing site. Her sisters soon caught up with her, and they all waited on the ledge.

A deep voice called out, "Ahoy there!"

[12] **rations**—*specific amounts of food*

"It's *Father*!" Abbie cried joyously.

"Father! Father!" the girls shouted as they scampered down the steps. Abbie caught the end of the rope he tossed and hauled the boat up on the ways.[13] As soon as he touched shore, they rushed to him, chattering all at once.

He turned to Abbie, and his voice choked. "I knew I'd find you all well and safe. Everyone in Rockland feared for your lives, but I told them this house would endure. And I knew you'd keep the lights burning, Daughter. They certainly welcomed me."

---

[13] **ways**—*structure on land from which a boat is launched*

"Oh, Father, it's so good to have you home!" was all she could say.

That evening the family gathered at the fireside, relishing the fresh milk and fruit Mr. Burgess had brought. Abbie put away the other supplies, her spirits light again. Her father was home; their larder[14] was full; and her mother had perked up a great deal already. Best of all, the granite house had weathered the storm.

According to the accounts her father brought from the mainland, it was one of the severest storms the old-timers could recollect. It had wreaked terrible damage to the waterfront at Rockland, and there'd been word of many disasters on the high seas. Because of its deep drifts of snow, sleet, and gales, mainlanders were already calling it the "winter of the tempests."

After a while, Abbie sat down at the kitchen table and began a letter to her friend in Rockland. She explained some of the events of the past weeks, and then added: "Though at times I was greatly exhausted from work, the lights did not fail once. Under God I was able to perform all my regular duties as well as my father's."

[14] **larder**—*pantry*

I WONDER . . .

1. Who was the multidimensional character in the story? Explain your answer.
2. Who was Mr. Burgess and what was the significance of his being away from home?
3. What might the author have used for a source in the writing of this true story?
4. Write the cause/effect or problem/solution for each of the events below.

Cause: When Abigail realized a storm was approaching,

Effect: ______________________________

Problem: A breaker crashed on the roof, threatening to flood the hen coop.

Solution: ______________________________

Problem: ______________________________

Solution: Abigail moved her family to the safety of the tower.

IN THE SPOTLIGHT
Mood

1. How did the author's choice of words at the beginning of the selection establish the mood?
2. How did Abbie's actions, in response to her fearful sisters, create a different mood?
3. How did the mood shift after the worst of the storm had passed?
4. How would you describe the mood at the end of this selection?

What would you do if you were in Abbie's situation? What did Abbie do to keep her courage up when things were difficult and dangerous?

Jesus and I

Dan Crawford

I cannot do it alone;
The waves run fast and high,
And the fogs close chill around,
And the light goes out in the sky;
But I know that we two
Shall win in the end—
Jesus and I.

I cannot row it myself,
My boat on the raging sea;
But beside me sits Another,
Who pulls or steers with me;
And I know that we two
Shall come safe into port—
His child and He.

Coward and wayward* and weak,
I change with the changing sky.
Today so eager and brave,
Tomorrow not caring to try;
But He never gives in,
So we two shall win—
Jesus and I.

* **wayward**—*doing the opposite of what is desired; obstinate*

Strong and tender and true,
Crucified once for me!
Never will He change, I know,
Whatever I may be!
But all He says I must do,
Is simply, "Trust in Me."
We shall finish our course
And reach home at last—
His child and He.

In the Spotlight

Figurative Language

1. In the second stanza, what metaphor does the poet use to describe his life on earth?
2. What does the port represent?

I WONDER . . .

1. How does the author's use of repetition reinforce the poet's message/theme?
2. Where has the poet placed his confidence?
3. Why does the poet believe his confidence is well-placed?

Onward and Onward

Abby Henry

Onward and onward the brave knights rode forth
Off to the battle that brewed in the north,
Hoping and wanting to each prove his worth,
Serving the King who ruled Heaven and Earth.

Backward and backward the knights fled away.
Defeat had fallen to them on that day.
Wearied and wounded, they trudged in dismay,
Fearing and fretting, what would the King say?

"Upward now, upward!" was the King's command.
"You're knights in My charge, soldiers of this land.
Though bruised and battered before Me you stand,
I have no complaints, no fierce reprimand."

"Forward and forward, My knights, you must go,
Even when failure dares to bring you low.
For there's a command I want you to know,
Something to cling to no matter the foe. . ."

When there's a struggle that you want to win,
A battle without, a trial within,
Think of the words of the King to His men:
"Though you may stumble, you must rise again."

In the Spotlight

Imagery and Symbolism

1. How does the author's use of repetition highlight the poem's theme?
2. Underline the poet's use of alliteration.
3. There is symbolism in this allegorical poem. Whom does the King represent, and who are the knights?
4. What are the knights fighting against?
5. How does the King encourage the knights?
6. What is the command the King wants the knights to remember?

Think on These Things

Throughout *More Than Conquerors*, we have seen hero after hero overcome fear, distraction, or doubt. The success of these characters has been highlighted and celebrated. But in many of our stories, the characters failed before they ever conquered. What might have happened had Hans given up after falling off Borina? Or if Punchinello and his friends had never returned to Eli and learned to be content? Thankfully, these characters did not quit—and we shouldn't either. Proverbs 24:16 tells us that "a just man falleth seven times, and riseth up again." We will make mistakes. We will stumble, fall, and even fail. Rather than giving in to discouragement or defeat, we must heed the command of our King to get back up and try again. Only then, with God's guidance and strength, can we truly conquer the struggles and obstacles before us.

In the Spotlight

Test Your Map Skills

Complete after "A Race Against Death" on page 11.

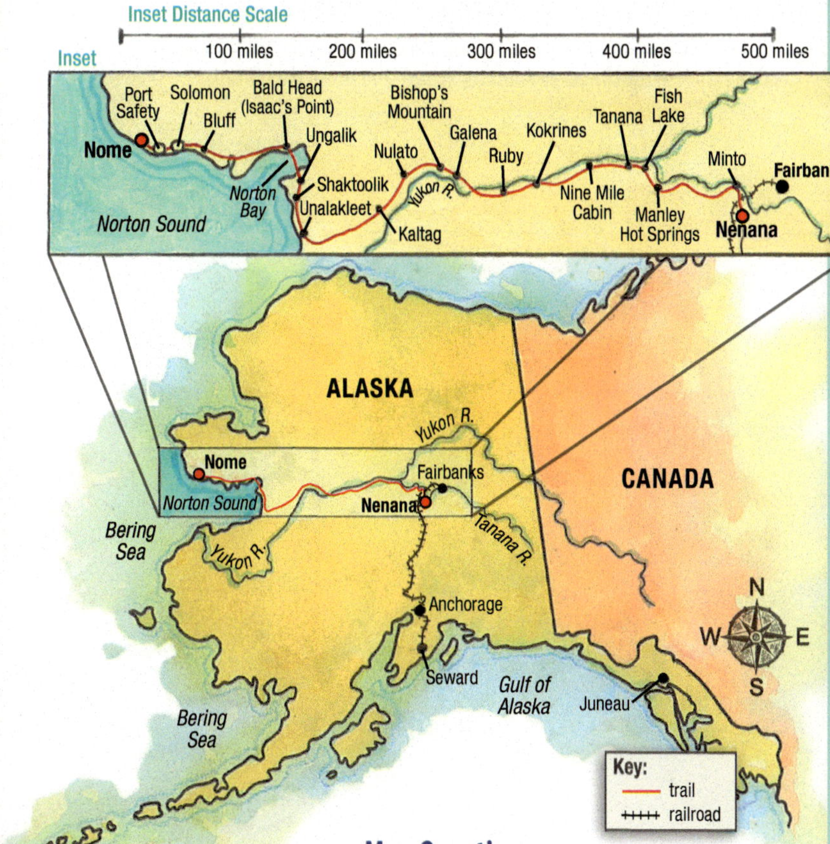

Map Questions

1. Which direction did the train travel when going from Anchorage to Nenana?
2. Which direction did the mushers travel when going from Nenana to Nome?
3. The length of the trail from Nenana to Nome was about 650 miles. If an airplane had been able to fly from Nenana to Nome, about how many miles would it have traveled? Explain the difference in distance.
   a. about 250 miles b. almost 500 miles
4. How many total miles did the antitoxin travel by land from Anchorage to Nome?
   a. less than 800 miles b. more than 900 miles
5. Which town did Seppala leave just before he crossed Norton Sound?
   a. Bald Head b. Golovin c. Shaktoolik d. Ungalik
6. What was the first town Seppala reached after crossing Norton Sound?
   a. Bald Head b. Golovin c. Shaktoolik d. Ungalik

In the Spotlight

Analyze the Character

Complete after "Ross Carson's Courage" on page 40.

Analyze the character of Ross Carson. List the character's traits and provide proof of the trait from the text along with the page number where the proof was found.

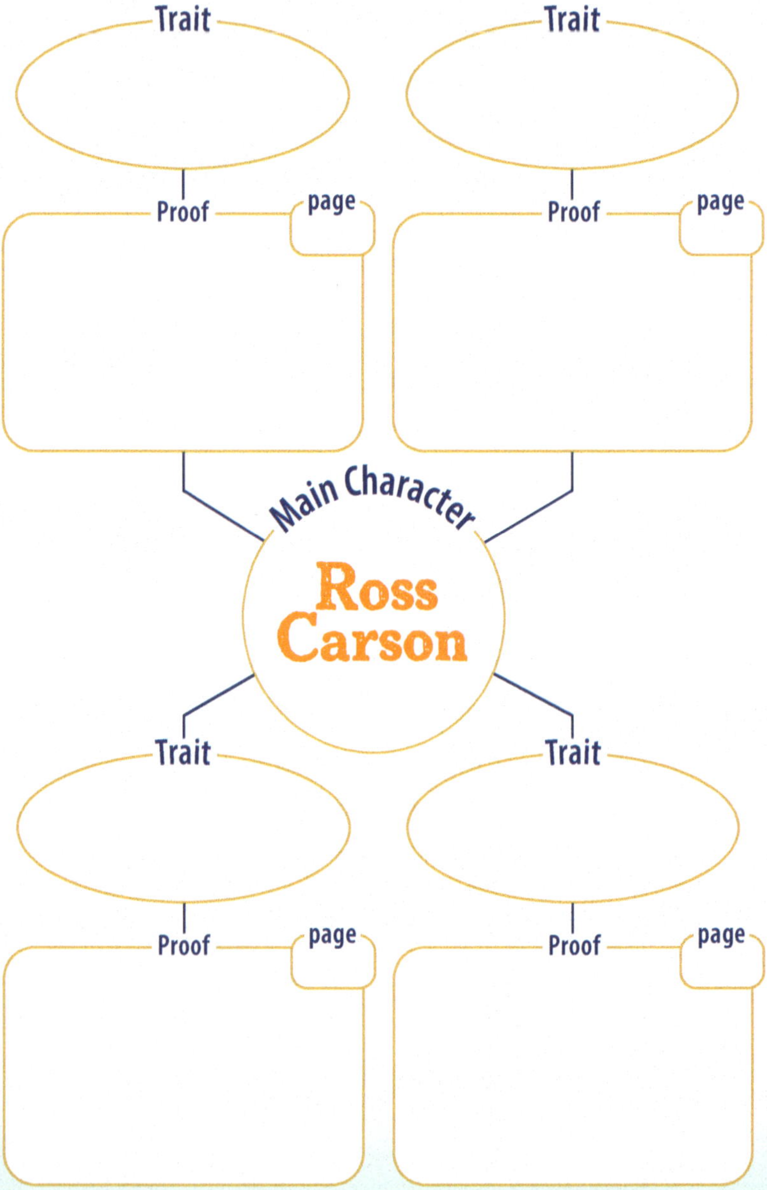

IN THE SPOTLIGHT

Analyze the Characters' Development

Complete after "The Case of the Perplexed Playwright" on page 66.

For each pair of characters, choose the one you believe is multidimensional and explain why.

1. Sophie or Lucas

2. Juan or Marcos

3. Theo or Rory

In the Spotlight

Write Creatively

Complete after "Be Still and Know: The Testimony of a Girl Who Gave Her Life to God" on page 157.

Consider the elements of a chronological text structure and write a biographical sketch about someone in your life whom you admire. Include simple illustrations in the space provided.

In the Spotlight

Analyze the Figurative Language

Complete after "He Is My Refuge" on page 184.

In the first stanza, several metaphors are used to describe the Lord. Use the metaphorical phrases to complete the wheel. The first two have been done for you.

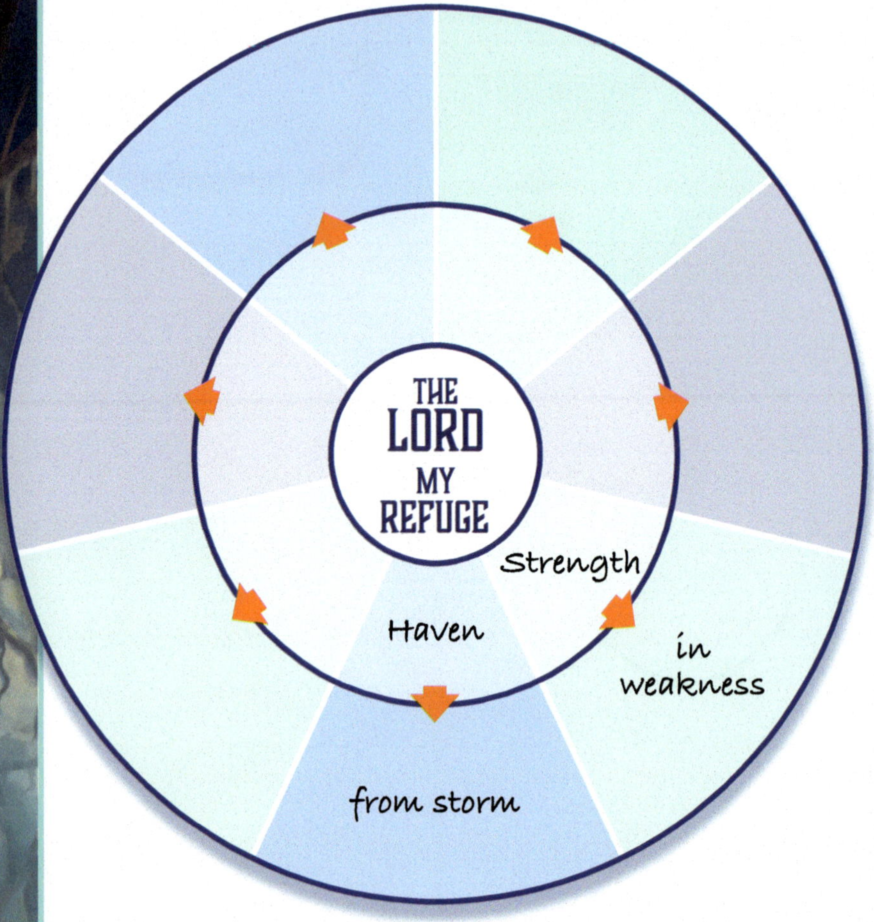

The Lord is my Refuge,	My Joy in all sorrow,
My Haven from storm,	My Hope in despair,
My Strength in all weakness,	My Courage in conquest,
My Peace in alarm,	My Helper in prayer.

CREDITS

Photo credits are listed in the order images appear on each page.

Cover–Elenasz/Depositphotos.com, Image by khaneeros on Freepik, Image by brgfx on Freepik, Image by rawpixel.com on Freepik, Abeka; Image and design elements used throughout–Image by lileonidp on Freepik, Image by dashadima on Freepik, Image by macrovector on Freepik, Image by Freepik (6), Image by Abuntdesign on Freepik, Image by gstudioimagen1 on Freepik, Image by khaneeros on Freepik, Image by brgfx on Freepik, Image by rawpixel.com on Freepik (3), Abeka; 3–Chiara Salvadora/Moment via Getty Images; 13–Image by 30031983q on Freepik; 27–Operation 2021/Alamy Stock Photo; 28, 35–Courtesy of the Air Force Historical Research Agency; 37–Leigh Green/Alamy Stock Photo; 39–jayk7/Moment via Getty Images; 65–ly86/Digital Vision Vectors via Getty Images; 107–guvendemir/E+ via Getty Images, debibishop/E+ via Getty Images; 108-117–Illustrations from *If Only I Had a Green Nose* text by Max Lucado, illustrations by Sergio Martinez. Copyright © 2002. Used by permission of Crossway, a publishing ministry of Good News Publishers, Wheaton, IL 60187, www.crossway.org All rights reserved.; 130–seanscott/RooM via Getty Images;131–Chris Jackson via Getty Images, Image by Rochak Shukla on Freepik, Nasha Photography/Moment via Getty Images; 132–Leon Neal via Getty Images; 133–Little Valleys/Alamy Stock Photo, Juniors Bildarchiv GmbH/Alamy Stock Photo, kpa/United Archives/Hulton Archives via Getty Images; 134–Gary Calton/Alamy Stock Photo; 148-149–ImagineGolf via Getty Images, Image by fetrinka on Freepik; 157-165–Image by rattikankeawpun on Freepik; 157–Len Trievnor/Express/Hulton Archive via Getty Images, Image by pikisuperstar on Freepik; 158–Image by alvaro_cabrera on Freepik; 161–Image by gstudioimagen on Freepik, Abeka, Image of Helen Roseveare with nursing students; 162–Image by arifeariburnu on Freepik; 164–Image by peterdraw.co on Freepik, Image of Helen Roseveare with a child; 166–Image by konstantinov–62 on Freepik; 167-170–courtesy of Ximena Porras Ramirez; 172-173–Image by watercolor_vect on Freepik; 173–ithinksky/DigitalVision Vectors via Getty Images, Wavebreakmedia/iStock via Getty Images; 174-175–Image by azerbaijan_stockers on Freepik(2), 174–Image by nndanko on Freepik, Image by EyeEm on Freepik; 175–Image by oxanadenezhkina on Freepik; 181–Image by daboost on Freepik; 184–Hubert Zegota/500px via Getty Images; 198–Mike Hill/Stone via Getty Images; 203–Image by 30031983q on Freepik.

Excerpt from *The Quest for Seven Castles* by Ed Dunlop, Copyright © 2006, book two in The Terrestria Chronicles. Reprinted with the permission of the author. All rights reserved.

Excerpts from *White Stallion of Lipizza* by Marguerite Henry from chapters titled "Between the Pillars" and "A Rascal in the Gallery." Copyright © 1964 by Rand McNally & Company. Reprinted with the permission of Aladdin, an imprint of Simon & Schuster Children's Publishing Division. All rights reserved.

"The Great Storm" adapted from chapter 15 of *Abbie Burgess: Lighthouse Heroine* by Dorothy Holder Jones and Ruth Sexton Sargent Copyright © 1969, 1999 and published by Lighthouse Digest, East Machias, ME, originally published by Funk & Wagnalls, a division of Reader's Digest Books, Inc. Reprinted by permission of Lighthouse Digest and the Estate of Ruth Sexton Sargent. All rights reserved.

If Only I Had a Green Nose by Max Lucado, illustrated by Sergio Martinez. Copyright © 2002. Used by permission of Crossway, a publishing ministry of Good News Publishers, Wheaton, IL 60187, www.crossway.org. All rights reserved.